The Charlatan

A play

William Norfolk

Samuel French - London
New York - Toronto - Hollywood

© 1991 BY WILLIAM NORFOLK

Rights of Performance by Amateurs are controlled by Samuel French Ltd, 52 Fitzroy Street, London W1P 6JR, and they, or their authorized agents, issue licences to amateurs on payment of a fee. **It is an infringement of the Copyright to give any performance or public reading of the play before the fee has been paid and the licence issued.**

The Royalty Fee indicated below is subject to contract and subject to variation at the sole discretion of Samuel French Ltd.

                      Basic fee for each and every
                      performance by amateurs   Code M
                      in the British Isles

The Professional Rights in this play are controlled by SAMUEL FRENCH LTD, 52 FITZROY STREET, LONDON W1P 6JR.

> **The publication of this play does not imply that it is necessarily available for performance by amateurs or professionals, either in the British Isles or Overseas. Amateurs and professionals considering a production are strongly advised in their own interests to apply to appropriate agents for consent before starting rehearsals or booking a theatre or hall.**

GIFT
NL000 11325

ISBN 0 573 01731 X

Please see page iv for further copyright information.

THE CHARLATAN

The world premiere of this play was given by the City Players of St Louis, Missouri, USA, when the cast was as follows:

Anton Mesmer	Rohn Thomas
Marie-Theresa Paradies	Susan Wells-Souza
Professor Barth	Wayne Richards
Doctor Stoerck	Bob Fowler
Frau Schwartz	Margie Gale
Herr Paradies	Jim Forquer
Frau Paradies	Johanna Ball
Frau Mesmer	Kate Wylie

The play directed by Carl Zimmerle

Production Stage Manager	Steve Hinson
Lighting design	John E. Owens
Music and sound design	Kristi Hervig
Costumer	David Clinton Parks
Properties Manager	Lizz Caplan
General Production Manager	Girard Tucker

COPYRIGHT INFORMATION

(See also page ii)

This play is fully protected under the Copyright Laws of the British Commonwealth of Nations, the United States of America and all countries of the Berne and Universal Copyright Conventions.

All rights, including Stage, Motion Picture, Radio, Television, Public Reading, and Translation into Foreign Languages, are strictly reserved.

No part of this publication may lawfully be reproduced in ANY form or by any means—photocopying, typescript, recording (including video-recording), manuscript, electronic, mechanical, or otherwise—or be transmitted or stored in a retrieval system, without prior permission.

Licences for amateur performances are issued subject to the understanding that it shall be made clear in all advertising matter that the audience will witness an amateur performance; that the names of the authors of the plays shall be included on all announcements and on all programmes; and that the integrity of the authors' work will be preserved.

The Royalty Fee is subject to contract and subject to variation at the sole discretion of Samuel French Ltd.

In Theatres or Halls seating Six Hundred or more the fee will be subject to negotiation.

In Territories Overseas the fee quoted in this Acting Edition may not apply. A fee will be quoted on application to our local authorized agent, or if there is no such agent, on application to Samuel French Ltd, London.

VIDEO RECORDING OF AMATEUR PRODUCTIONS

Please note that the copyright laws governing video-recording are extremely complex and that it should not be assumed that any play may be video-recorded *for whatever purpose* without first obtaining the permission of the appropriate agents. The fact that a play is published by Samuel French Ltd does not indicate that video rights are available or that Samuel French Ltd controls such rights.

CHARACTERS

Anton Mesmer
Maria-Theresa Paradies
Professor Barth
Doctor Stoerck
Frau Schwartz
Herr Paradies
Frau Paradies
Frau Mesmer

SYNOPSIS OF SCENES

PROLOGUE	Paris 1784. The Tuilleries. Evening
ACT I	Vienna 1777. Frau Schwartz's coffee house, the residences of the Mesmers and the Paradies
ACT II	The same
EPILOGUE	Paris 1784. A continuation of the Prologue

Other plays by William Norfolk, published by Samuel French Ltd, are:

**The Lights Are Warm and Coloured
Hunting Pink
Nine Floors Not Counting the Mezzanine
Old Quebec
We've Minds of Our Own**

PROLOGUE

Paris, 1784. The Tuilleries. Evening

Preceding the rise of the CURTAIN *the final bars of Mozart's Piano Concerto No. 18 in B flat, K456, are heard, followed by applause*

Mesmer, a man of fifty, heavily cloaked, stands in the shadow of the trees

Maria-Theresa Paradies, an attractive woman of twenty-five, enters, also cloaked, and feeling her way with an elegant cane. Her step is purposeful, yet she suddenly stops, aware of Mesmer's presence, and stands motionless

Maria (*hoarsely*) Doctor Mesmer!

He makes no reply. She appears about to continue walking, but stays

Don't be afraid. I'm quite harmless. I no longer have convulsions, or scream.

Pause

You can't harm me, either. I'm quite self-sufficient nowadays. You heard me play. And before their Royal Highnesses, too. Marie-Antoinette even called out to me, "Bravo, Mam'selle Paradies!" I hope I did the composer justice. Herr Mozart dedicated the concerto to me. But I suppose you knew that, being a friend of the family?

Mesmer You played excellently, Fräulein. I'm sure Wolferl would have been proud of you, had he been able to attend.

Pause

Maria How formal you sound. Are you lurking in the shadows? You can come out, you know. I can't see you.

Mesmer Are you taunting me?

Maria (*with great self-control*) The voice ... just the same as I remembered it ... after all these years.

Mesmer Seven, to be precise.

Maria You would have to be precise, of course. An eventful seven years, Doctor.

Mesmer For both of us. I've followed your progress.

Maria And I yours.

Pause

Why should I taunt you for being as I am? What would I have become, had I kept my sight? Someone's maid? A seamstress?

Mesmer There was more at stake than your mere livelihood.

Maria For whom?
Mesmer For both of us.

Pause

Maria I didn't understand the politics of the situation at the time. I thought you simply wanted to give a poor blind girl back her sight. *Quelle naïveté!*
Mesmer How cynical you've become.
Maria (*smiling*) Realistic. We're living in the age of reason, Doctor. You had something to prove.
Mesmer I did prove it.
Maria Not to the medical faculty of Vienna. You wanted to show them that your claims were justified, and that your animal-magnetism was a miraculous healer, didn't you? I was merely a ... a means to an end. An end that proved to be a scandal and a fiasco.
Mesmer You were able to see when you left me.

Pause

Maria That's true. I'm not being fair. Your claims were just. You were able to make me see. At least ... *physically* ... you made me see *things*. Frankly, I've always seen more clearly in the dark. Isn't that ironic? But you wouldn't understand. How could you? You've always had your sight.
Mesmer The medical faculty consisted of men with sight, but not one of them could see. It's true, I wanted to prove my theory to them, but you were never just "a means to an end", Fräulein. You were someone who needed my help, and I gave it to you, as I've given it to others who needed it. What does it matter if there were ... further considerations in your case?
Frau Paradies (*off*) Maria-Theresa!
Maria There's Mother.
Mesmer Is she still as unreasonable?
Maria (*laughing*) She's threatened to cut off your head should she ever see you again. But she and Papa are bound to worry. In those days they had only a handicapped daughter to lose. Now they've a celebrated pianist.
Mesmer Lose?
Maria They've become accustomed to a more luxurious standard of living. Everywhere I'm announced as "the blind pianist". It proves quite an attraction. After all, the world is full of pianists who can see.
Frau Paradies (*off, more impatiently*) Maria-Theresa!
Mesmer Do you never feel——?
Maria Don't worry about me. I'm perfectly happy. Really.

Pause. She smiles

Besides, if you took away my blindness, what could you offer me in return?

The Lights fade

ACT I

Vienna, January 1777

The set consists of three acting areas. Centre, Frau Schwartz's coffee house. To the right and left of this, the residences of the Mesmers and the Paradies

The Lights are up on the coffee house, where Doctor Stoerck and Professor Barth play piquet. Stoerck deals. Frau Schwartz fetches them brandy

Barth Where are all your customers, Frau Schwartz?
Frau Schwartz (*shrugging*) On such a cold January evening, Professor, they prefer to huddle round their fires, I suppose.

She goes

Barth That was a fine dinner, Anton.
Stoerck I didn't want to spoil it, so invited Mesmer to drop in here to meet us. He doesn't care for this "gossip shop", as he calls it, so won't stay for long.
Barth (*arranging cards*) He certainly does lecture.
Stoerck He calls it conversation.
Barth I'm exchanging three cards. (*He places three from his hand face-down on the table, and picks up three from the stock-pile*)
Stoerck Have you ever tried altering the direction of the conversation when he's on about his "animal-magnetism"? It's like trying to stop an avalanche. I'm exchanging five. (*Same procedure as Barth, except with five cards*) An evening of his theorizing would have ruined my appetite. That's why I thought it advisable not to ask him to dinner.
Barth You were great friends at one time, weren't you? Point of six.
Stoerck Good.
Barth Quint to the ace.
Stoerck Good. Friends since his university days.
Barth Three aces.
Stoerck Not good.
Barth Six and fifteen. Twenty-one. (*He plays a card*) Twenty-two.
Stoerck Fourteen. I was a witness at his wedding, as a matter of fact. Charming woman. A widow, she was.
Barth And wealthy, I believe. Twenty-three.
Stoerck However, as personal physician to the Empress, I can't afford to be too involved with practitioners of these ... medical novelties.

He plays a card. Barth picks up a trick and leads a card

Barth Twenty-four. His theory is certainly very novel.
Stoerck But you, too, have yet to be convinced of its medical value?

He plays a card. Barth picks up a trick and leads a card

Barth Twenty-five. He's too theatrical.
Stoerck It's made him notorious.
Barth Or famous, depending on one's point of view.
Stoerck (*playing a card*) It reflects on the medical faculty.

Barth picks up a trick and leads a card

Barth Twenty-six.
Stoerck (*playing a card*) We celebrated my appointment as president of the faculty together. Oh, must have been . . . five years ago? He was infinitely better company in those days.

Barth picks up a trick and leads a card

Barth Twenty-seven.
Stoerck The whole idea of these . . . magical powers . . . smacks too much of the occult for my taste.

He plays a card. Barth takes a trick and leads a card

Barth Twenty-eight. Ingenhousz said almost the same thing, apparently.
Stoerck And Ingenhousz was merely a sceptic, you know, until Mesmer invited him along to one of his . . . performances.

He plays a card. Barth takes a trick and leads a card

Barth Twenty-nine. The case of Fräulein Oesterlin?
Stoerck You heard the story?
Barth Several versions. Which had you in mind?
Stoerck The horse's mouth.

He plays a card. Barth takes a trick and leads a card

Barth Thirty. Ingenhousz?
Stoerck The very same. It seems the young woman in question had been ill for many years. Hysterical fever . . . convulsions . . . despondency . . . hallucinations. As Ingenhousz so aptly put it, "not so much a set of symptoms as a list of the plagues of Egypt". (*He plays a card, picks up a trick*) Now I've forgotten what my score was.
Barth Fourteen.
Stoerck Fourteen. Fifteen. (*He leads a card*) Sixteen.
Barth She lived with the Mesmers, didn't she?

He plays a card. Stoerck takes a trick and leads a card

Stoerck Seventeen. Possibly a relative, of some sort, on his side. His stepson later married her. However, he'd been treating her, and he invited Ingenhousz over for one of his healing sessions.
Barth Which, I believe, Ingenhousz leapt at?

He plays a card. Stoerck takes a trick and leads a card

Stoerck Eighteen.

Act I

Barth Thirty and ten for me. Forty.

Stoerck jots down the score and gives the cards to Barth to shuffle

Stoerck Naturally. As I said earlier, he was a sceptic in those days ... and, not being a member of the faculty, not part of the great conspiracy that Mesmer imagines to be maligning his great gift to the world.

Barth (*smiling*) A disciple in embryo? Cut.

Stoerck cuts the cards, and Barth deals

Stoerck Mesmer may have thought so. Anyway, when Ingenhousz arrived, the poor woman was lying on the bed, completely still. He told Ingenhousz, "She will wake only when I wish her to; she will react only to my magnetism", or some such dialogue. He then moved to the bed and touched her head and arms lightly with his fingertips. Apparently she shuddered, and her whole body jerked as though in pain. She became calm only when he moved his hand above her—not touching her—from head to foot. Ingenhousz tried similar actions, but nothing happened. Mesmer then crowed, "You see? Only I can make her move!" and proceeded with his next coloratura aria.

Barth He passed on some of his magnetism, so I heard, by stroking Ingenhousz's hands, and when he repeated his previous aborted experiment, he now got a reaction from the lady?

Stoerck Oh, Mesmer has a good technique. He's simply in the wrong profession.

Barth What was the business with the six cups?

Stoerck He magnetized them.

Barth All six?

Stoerck And spoil the dramatic effect? No. He began by magnetizing only one.

Barth How?

Stoerck By placing both hands around it. He then touched the woman's hands with each of the cups in turn, and she cried out—as if burned—when she felt the one he had magnetized. Having created his effect, he placed that cup to one side and handed one to Ingenhousz that had not been magnetized, inviting him to touch the woman's hand with it. He did so, and, of course, nothing happened. So Mesmer told him to do so again—except that this time he held Ingenhousz's other hand—and, lo, the woman reacted as though in great pain.

Barth He passed the magnetism on to Ingenhousz?

Stoerck That was certainly the impression he intended.

Barth (*looking at the cards*) You to call.

Stoerck I'm exchanging four. (*He does so*) Then came the grand finale. Mesmer took a few steps from the bed—I can well imagine the great dramatic flourish—and pointed imperiously at the poor wretch, who writhed as if in great agony. The moment he stopped pointing, she stopped writhing.

Barth I'm exchanging three. (*He does so*) And that was the end of the demonstration?

Stoerck And resist a burst of fireworks? Point of six.
Barth Good.
Stoerck Tierce to the ace.
Barth Not good.
Stoerck Three aces.
Barth Good.
Stoerck That's six and three and three. Twelve. (*He plays a card*) Thirteen. He then repeated the pointing episode, except that this time he had Ingenhousz stand between him and the woman, just to prove that his power could go through, or round, Ingenhousz. Then, a slight hesitation, as if waiting for applause, and the demonstration was over.
Barth (*playing a card*) How did Ingenhousz react?
Stoerck (*taking a trick, playing a card*) Fourteen. Like someone leaving the opera. In a dream, his head full of music and magic. And, talking of opera, it's not surprising that Mesmer's so dramatic—after all, he does have a private theatre in his gardens. Put on a new opera by the Mozart child a few years ago. I didn't see it. Prefer Gluck, personally. Anyway, Ingenhousz soon returned to his scepticism. You know how it is. The head clears, one returns to terra firma.
Barth (*playing a card*) Mesmer used no magnets for his performance?
Stoerck (*taking a trick, playing a card*) Fifteen. Not on this occasion. He does use them. Ingenhousz, himself, uses them in prescribed cases. But this was a gala performance. Look! No hands!

Pause

There was one slight irony to the situation. Ingenhousz swears he had some magnets in his pockets that day—by accident, it seems—and insists they caused the effects that he saw.
Barth (*playing a card*) How careless of him.
Stoerck (*taking a trick, playing a card*) Sixteen. Inhospitable, I'd have said. Rather like taking one's own food to a banquet.

Mesmer enters

Sorry to bring you out on so cold an evening.
Mesmer I've no doubt it's of immense importance. (*To Barth*) And how are you, Joseph?
Barth Winning.
Stoerck He chatters, so that I lose count.
Mesmer It came as something of a surprise, hearing from you. We see so little of each other these days.
Stoerck The Empress keeps me busy at Court.
Mesmer Ah, of course. The Empress.
Stoerck Sit down, Anton. It is good to see you. Have some brandy.
Mesmer I'm afraid there isn't time to be social. I have a patient to attend. So, if you could please tell me why you asked me here . . .? Unless, of course, it was to watch you losing at piquet? (*He remains standing*)
Stoerck There's someone I'd like you to see.
Mesmer Professionally?

Act I

Stoerck A difficult case.
Mesmer But you don't believe in my method.
Stoerck Her father, seemingly, does.
Mesmer Poor, misguided fool. Do I know him?
Stoerck Herr Paradies. He's a secretary at the Court, and his daughter——
Mesmer Yes, yes. I've heard her play the pianoforte. She's blind——
Barth Since she was three years old. Woke up one morning, blind. I'll be frank with you, Mesmer. I think it's hopeless.
Mesmer Then why send her to me?
Stoerck It's the Empress's idea. She's always taken an interest in the girl, and when Paradies took up the matter with her . . .
Barth Well, you have achieved a certain degree of fame with regard to unusual cases . . .
Mesmer Fame? Or disrepute?
Stoerck (*laughing*) You listen to too much gossip.
Mesmer (*wryly*) It gets reported back to me by well-meaning friends. But you're an eye-specialist, Joseph, and if you can't do anything . . .?
Barth All the orthodox methods have been tried. Leeches, blisters, cauterization . . .
Stoerck Her head was encased in plaster for two months——
Barth But to no avail.
Mesmer (*heavily*) She's still alive, I take it?
Stoerck (*smiling*) She has great spirit.
Mesmer Is her blindness caused by organic effect?
Barth We think not.

The scene dims, and the Lights come up on a room in the Paradies household. Maria-Theresa sits playing the piano softly

   Her father enters, carrying a book

Herr Paradies (*whispering*) That's beautiful, Maria. Take no notice of me. (*He sits and listens for a moment, then commences to read his book*)

Maria continues playing

   A moment later her mother bustles in. Both parents are in their forties

Frau Paradies That's a pretty piece, dear. (*She plumps cushions and re-arranges flowers*) Is there anything I can get for you, Maria?
Maria (*patiently*) No, thank you, Mama.
Frau Paradies Some hot chocolate, perhaps?
Maria No, thank you, Mama.
Frau Paradies Nothing at all?

Maria stops playing

Maria No, thank you, Mama.
Herr Paradies (*not looking up from his book*) Leave the girl alone.
Frau Paradies What did you say?
Herr Paradies You heard me.

Maria begins to play

Frau Paradies That's how much your father cares about you. Sometimes I wonder——
Herr Paradies Isn't there anything that needs doing in any of the other rooms? The girl's trying to practise.

Maria stops playing

Maria I'm perfectly all right, Mama. Really.
Frau Paradies You always say that.
Herr Paradies Yet you persist in disturbing her.
Frau Paradies But she's not all right. You know it, and I——
Herr Paradies She would be, if you'd leave her alone.
Frau Paradies You're an unfeeling monster. Here we are, with a daughter so ... afflicted ... and you won't even take your nose out of that book to——
Herr Paradies I'm trying to arrange for her to see Mesmer, aren't I?
Frau Paradies Against my better judgement.
Herr Paradies I've learned, from experience, that your better judgement's highly suspect. If you spent less time listening to the silly chatter of your cronies——
Frau Paradies The man's a charlatan. Everyone knows it. How you can place my poor baby in his hands I shall never——
Herr Paradies Your "poor baby" happens to be eighteen years old, and——
Frau Paradies Under other circumstances——
Herr Paradies Under any circumstances, she'd still be eighteen years old. Except she'd probably have broken free of this ... smothering you subject her to!
Frau Paradies You don't have an iota of feeling for her, do you? Not one——
Herr Paradies She's perfectly happy when she plays the piano, so why don't——?

Maria bangs discordantly on the keys

Maria Will you stop talking about me in the third person, as though I were an idiot child!
Frau Paradies Now, don't upset yourself——
Maria I'm not upsetting myself. You're upsetting me, Mama. Continually upsetting me. Why don't you leave me alone?
Frau Paradies (*tight-lipped*) That's the sort of thanks you get for years of devotion ... sacrifice ... A fine state you'd be in if I did leave you to your own devices. Falling about in fits ... stumbling over things ... (*More softly*) We love you, darling, and that's why we're so concerned for you ...

Pause

Maria Sorry, Mama. I know.
Frau Paradies We do our best ...

Maria begins playing again

Act I

Are you sure you wouldn't like some chocolate? It would help calm your nerves.

She stops playing

Maria (*resignedly*) Very well, Mama. Make me some hot chocolate.
Frau Paradies You don't sound very sure.
Maria I'm quite sure.
Frau Paradies I mean, if you don't really want it ...
Maria (*patiently*) But I do want it.
Frau Paradies You don't need to humour me.
Herr Paradies It's usually the only way to silence you.
Frau Paradies No-one's talking to you. (*To Maria*) Well?

Maria ignores her, and begins playing very fast, and very loudly

Maria-Theresa! I'm talking to you!

She continues playing, becoming more erratic as the scene continues

You're a wretched, ungrateful girl!
Herr Paradies Is that what you want? Gratitude? To see her grovelling?
Frau Paradies You certainly do little enough for her.
Herr Paradies I treat her as a normal adult.
Frau Paradies She's not a normal adult.
Herr Paradies You won't allow her to be.
Frau Paradies Were it not for my constant attention, where would she be?
Herr Paradies Far happier, I imagine.
Frau Paradies You do nothing——
Herr Paradies Were it not for the bursary the Empress allows her, where would she be? I got that for her.
Frau Paradies Oh, it's easy enough, handing out money, and letting your responsibility end there.
Herr Paradies We would never have been able to afford her music lessons.
Frau Paradies A little warmth from her father——
Herr Paradies A little less slow strangulation from her mother——
Frau Paradies Not so loud, Maria.
Herr Paradies (*acidly*) We can hardly hear ourselves shout.

Maria ignores them, and continues playing

Frau Paradies You see? She takes no notice of anything I say. She needs the authority of a father to keep her under control.
Herr Paradies She'd be perfectly all right, if left alone.

The playing suddenly stops. Maria begins swaying from side to side, then her limbs start to jerk, and she makes hoarse guttural sounds

Frau Paradies Now see what you've done!

They rush to her, and her father catches her just as she is about to topple from the stool. He lowers her to the floor, where she remains making sounds and twitching

My poor baby. You see, we can't leave you alone for a minute.

The Lights dim and come up again on the scene with Mesmer, Barth and Stoerck

Stoerck As Joseph told you, she was perfectly all right until she was three years old. It happened overnight.

Pause

Well? Will you see her?

Pause

Mesmer And if I fail to cure her?
Barth (*shrugging*) We failed.
Mesmer That hardly consoles me. You tried nothing new. You failed by orthodox methods, and people can accept that. Failure by me would have the whole of Vienna smugly whispering that my animal-magnetism is just a passing novelty, like every elixir of life peddled by every trickster they ever knew.
Stoerck Is your vanity all that matters?
Mesmer My reputation, not my vanity. You see, difficult though you may find it to believe, there are those who actually trust in me and my "unorthodox" method. I need to retain their belief. When you fail, people merely shrug their shoulders—if, indeed, they ever get to hear of it—but when I fail, the whole of Vienna learns of it. Frau Schwartz sees to that!
Stoerck Then you won't accept the——?
Mesmer (*wryly*) Challenge?
Stoerck I was about to say "the case". But "challenge" will do, unless you disapprove of the term.
Mesmer Its usage. When people refer to something being "a challenge" it generally implies one is being dared to do it!
Stoerck (*smiling*) It's a substitute for lack of argument.

Pause

Well?

Pause

Mesmer Very well. Get her father to bring her along, and if there's no organic defect I'll see what I can do. (*He turns to go*) There is, however, one condition ...
Stoerck Of course.
Mesmer If I am successful, I want her officially presented at Court.
Stoerck It will be arranged. In fact, the Empress will no doubt insist upon it. After all, she has always shown great concern regarding the welfare of Fräulein Paradies.

Mesmer begins to move off

And we could hardly deny you your moment of triumph.

Act I

Mesmer turns

Mesmer You miss the point, Anton. If I can cure the girl's blindness—who knows?—I may even be able to cure that of the Court and the medical faculty.

He goes

Barth I find his arrogance insufferable.
Stoerck How else can you face the ridicule ... the jibes ... the incredulity? It's his armour.
Barth "You failed by orthodox methods, and people can accept that!" Does he seriously expect the whole of Vienna to offer itself as a sacrifice to his experiments?
Stoerck Of course. Have you never suffered the throes of a bout of fanaticism?
Barth Never!
Stoerck A pity. It's most exhilarating. Of course, it has its after-effects. Like drinking too much wine.
Barth You think he'll get over it?
Stoerck I doubt it. Opposition only makes him more determined. Even his dubious successes he sees as monumental triumphs. Of course, this time it could be a real triumph for him ... since it would bring him to the attention of their Majesties.
Barth The Fräulein will really be presented at Court?
Stoerck If he's successful.
Barth But he won't be, will he?
Stoerck It's rather unlikely. Furthermore, my dear Joseph, he'd better not be. How would it appear if the Empress were to find he'd succeeded where her eye-specialist had failed? And with "unorthodox" methods, too. (*He smiles*)

The Lights dim and come up on Mesmer's study. He and Herr Paradies are seated

Mesmer Why did you not bring her?
Herr Paradies She's outside, in the carriage. I felt I'd like to talk to you first.
Mesmer I know the essential details regarding your daughter.
Herr Paradies But I don't know the essential details regarding your treatment.
Mesmer You nevertheless brought her to me.
Herr Paradies I've heard excellent reports of your work.
Mesmer You surprise me, Herr Paradies. I thought myself merely her last hope.
Herr Paradies The case of Fräulein Oesterlin——
Mesmer Ah! Dear Franzl! But I thought my success in that affair had been totally discredited by Ingenhousz and friends?
Herr Paradies Not entirely.
Mesmer How gratifying to learn there remains a tiny enlightened spot somewhere in this dark city. What do you wish to know of my method?

Herr Paradies Well ... what is ... "animal-magnetism"?
Mesmer "A certain subtle spirit"—to quote that great Englishman, Newton—pervading all material bodies by the force of which they attract each other. Magnetism. Hence, when related to living creatures, I term it "animal-magnetism". And this spirit—or fluid, as I prefer, since I believe it to be a fluid, undetectable to the human eye—has a rhythm analogous to the tides of the ocean. Similarly, it ebbs and it flows, and when disturbed, and out of harmony with the universal rhythm, nervous or mental disorders arise. This I base upon the premise that it enters the very substance of the nerves and affects them.
Herr Paradies But Maria-Theresa's blindness——
Mesmer I believe it to be a nervous disorder. Therefore, I believe——
Herr Paradies I'm sorry for the interruptions, but——
Mesmer So am I. This——
Herr Paradies Pardon me, Doctor, but please understand that for me this is something quite new and revolutionary——
Mesmer Naturally. And for all of Vienna. Nevertheless——
Herr Paradies What causes impediments in the flow?
Mesmer A variety of things. It can be influenced by the earth ... the heavenly bodies ... other living creatures ... All have a mutual influence that set up a ... natural balance. They can, however, occasionally be upset. And when that upset occurs we have what we call nervous disorder. Your daughter's blindness, for instance.
Herr Paradies Then how do you restore that balance?
Mesmer Fortunately, the fluid can be transferred from one person to another, and in this way it is possible to remove the blockage, and continue the flow. Not that everyone is capable of transferring the fluid, but it is my good fortune to be capable of doing so.
Herr Paradies With magnets? I've heard magnets are used.
Mesmer Sometimes a patient responds more quickly if I use something physical, like a magnet. Usually I simply transfer some of my own magnetism. Mind you, not all are susceptible to receiving it.
Herr Paradies And if they are not susceptible?
Mesmer (*shrugging*) More gossip for Vienna. You must have heard of my failures? If not, I'm sure Frau Schwartz has them itemized, and will be only too delighted to run through her repertoire. (*He rings a small bell*) And now I think it time to meet your daughter.
Herr Paradies I'll go——
Mesmer My wife will fetch her. However, before she does, there is something I feel should be made clear. If I decide to accept the Fräulein for treatment, I shall require that she stay here as my guest.
Herr Paradies Oh, but my wife wasn't expecting that. Could she not——?
Mesmer It is a prerequisite of her cure, since only under such conditions can I be held responsible for her overall mental and physical progress.

Frau Mesmer enters

Maria Anna, Herr Paradies.
Herr Paradies It's a pleasure ... (*He stands, and kisses her hand*)

Act I

Frau Mesmer Thank you, Herr Paradies. Were it not for the occasional kissing of my hand, I'd soon become convinced I'm a servant. Some day I'll push that bell up his nostril.
Mesmer Excuse the vulgarity; her father was an army officer.
Frau Mesmer He says that as if there were a world of difference in their chosen careers. As I see it, they both interfere in the normal pattern of life and death, with roughly the same ratio of success. However, I hope my husband can do something for your poor daughter. She has much promise as a pianist.
Mesmer She's outside, in a carriage. Will you fetch her in, please, dear?
Frau Mesmer (*curtsying*) Certainly, Herr Doctor.

She goes

Herr Paradies A charming woman. Apparently, as a hostess at your parties, she's the toast of Vienna.
Mesmer Her parties. And she calls them soirées. There's a subtle difference, I believe. The food bills are enormous. Maybe that's the difference.

Pause—then, suddenly

How is the relationship between your wife and yourself?
Herr Paradies I do not consider that relevant——
Mesmer Are we, or are we not, interested in the welfare of your daughter?
Herr Paradies Yes. But my private life is of no——
Mesmer Let me be the judge of that.

Pause

Well?

Pause

Herr Paradies Normal.
Mesmer Do you beat her?
Herr Paradies Of course not!
Mesmer Some would consider the beating of their wives quite normal. Do you dress her up in furs, and ride her as though she were a donkey?
Herr Paradies (*shocked*) Doctor!
Mesmer (*smiling*) An amusing confidence I once had from an elephantine countess. (*Reflectively*) "Normal." Now, what do you deem to be normal?
Herr Paradies (*shrugging*) You know.
Mesmer If I knew, Herr Paradies, I should not be wasting your time, and mine, by asking.
Herr Paradies You're a brusque man, Doctor.
Mesmer And you, sir, an evasive one.

Pause

Herr Paradies Occasionally we quarrel . . .
Mesmer Occasionally?

Pause

Herr Paradies Frequently.
Mesmer How frequently?

Pause

Herr Paradies Is this really——?
Mesmer It has already been established that my method is a trifle ... unorthodox. Therefore, accept this as one of my eccentricities, and answer my questions.
Herr Paradies My wife is always ... very tense ... and very protective toward Maria-Theresa, and this causes——
Mesmer What is your attitude?
Herr Paradies My daughter is stronger than her mother suspects.
Mesmer Good.
Herr Paradies (*surprised*) Our quarrelling?
Mesmer Her strength.

Frau Mesmer enters, holding Maria-Theresa by the arm. The girl is very nervous

Come in, Fräulein. (*He stands*) From this point, Herr Paradies, your role in your daughter's life is a purely passive one. You will be allowed to see her only by appointment, when I consider fit. Until such time——
Maria (*groping for him*) Papa!

They embrace

Herr Paradies He is a good man, Maria. Trust him.
Mesmer You do not know that I am a "good man", as you so glibly express it. You merely hope so.
Frau Mesmer The modesty of the man!
Mesmer (*ignoring her*) To the contrary, my reputation is anything but "good". However, I am honest, and if I think your daughter incurable, I shall soon inform you of the fact.
Maria (*to her father*) If you say he is good, Papa, I will try——
Herr Paradies Of course you will, liebchen.
Mesmer Enough of the sad farewells. After all, it's not that sad an occasion. Maria-Anna, see Herr Paradies to the door, please. I'm anxious to learn more about the Fräulein. Alone.
Herr Paradies I'd just like to thank you——
Mesmer For what? We don't even know that I'm able to do anything for her. (*To his wife*) Have you prepared a room for the Fräulein?
Maria (*frightened*) I'm to stay here?
Frau Mesmer Don't worry, child. You will be very——
Maria Must I? Must I, Papa? Couldn't I——?
Herr Paradies The doctor insists.
Mesmer Absolutely.

Pause—then, pointedly

So, that's settled. Goodbye, Herr Paradies. I'll send someone with a message when there is anything to report.

Act I

Herr Paradies (*kissing his daughter*) All will be well.

He goes quickly, followed by Frau Mesmer

Maria stands very still, clenching and unclenching her hands. Mesmer leads her to a window. She flinches at his touch

Mesmer I'm simply going to look at your eyes.

He does so, then leads her to the piano, and seats her on the stool. She reaches out and feels the keys. She is still very tense

Maria What are you going to do to me, Doctor? I'd rather know. Somehow the pain isn't quite so bad if I'm prepared for it.

She shudders. Mesmer seats himself close to her, where he can watch her reactions

Mesmer I'd like you to play something for me.
Maria I don't think I could stand a plaster cast again. Two months I was in it, so they told me. It seemed like years. I couldn't sleep...
Mesmer There'll be no plaster cast... nor electric shocks. Play something.

She begins to play and, after a few bars, begins to loosen up a little

Where would we be without music?

She continues playing throughout the ensuing dialogue

Are your parents fond of music?

Pause

Maria They like to hear me play.
Mesmer That doesn't answer my question, does it?

Pause

Maria They want to see me famous.
Mesmer Why?

Pause

Maria For my sake, I suppose. The money.
Mesmer And you?

Pause

Maria (*shyly*) I like the applause.

Pause

Mesmer Are you happy at home?
Maria What an absurd question. (*After a pause*) No, it's not an absurd question. It's the answer that was absurd. I don't know. (*She pauses*) I sometimes feel like a doll they're fighting over. (*She pauses*) Doctors don't usually talk to me. They just grunt, and bring out their instruments of...
Mesmer Torture?

Maria Is that disrespectful?
Mesmer (*smiling*) They're not all worthy of respect.

Pause

Maria They meant well.
Mesmer I'd hate to have that on my tombstone. "Here lies Mesmer—he meant well."
Maria (*a fleeting smile*) That wasn't what I said.
Mesmer Cynicism is the art of reinterpretation. Why did you say you felt like a doll?
Maria They each love me in a different kind of way.
Mesmer And each other?
Maria (*defensively*) Of course! (*After a pause*) I mean, everyone quarrels, don't they? From time to time. (*She pauses*) It's usually about me. In fact, were it not for me ... (*She pauses*) Things are better when I go on a concert tour ... just Mama and me ... when she has me all to herself. (*She stops playing*) You haven't told me what you're going to do with me.

Pause

Mesmer I'm going to do all within my power to show you the wonderful things that exist outside of your head.
Maria (*doubtfully*) Everyone gives the impression I'm missing a great deal ...

Pause

They don't seem to understand that music can be one's whole world ... one's whole existence ...

The scene dims, and the Lights come up on the Paradies house. Herr Paradies is reading a letter, while his wife bustles about fussing with cushions and so forth

Herr Paradies Stop fussing, and sit down.
Frau Paradies Servants simply aren't observant any more. The pink cushion used to be over there, and that one——
Herr Paradies I've never noticed, and I've been imprisoned here for twenty years, so why should a new servant——
Frau Paradies (*snorting*) Imprisoned! At least you're at the Court during the day. I never get a moment out——
Herr Paradies Except for an incredible number of cups of coffee with your vitriolic friends at the——
Frau Paradies Which reminds me——
Herr Paradies It would. Don't you want to know what's in the letter?
Frau Paradies Do you honestly think he's going to succeed where the real doctors failed?
Herr Paradies He says——
Frau Paradies If there's any genuine progress, why can't we go to see her?
Herr Paradies It was a condition——
Frau Paradies Frau Schwartz said——

Act I

Herr Paradies Wretched woman. If her pastries were half as fanciful as her chatter the shop would never be empty. Do you, or do you not, want to...?

Frau Paradies Very well. (*She sits*) Though I shan't believe a word of what he says!

Herr Paradies (*reading*) "... the next day she became——"

Frau Paradies After all, she's been there eight days. Usually, by this time——

Herr Paradies Do you find it absolutely impossible to keep quiet for two minutes?

Frau Paradies If you want me to creep around the house like a mute——

Herr Paradies It's a very ambitious idea, but I don't think you'll ever achieve it. (*Reading*) "... the next day she became hot and flushed, and her body trembled violently. This was the crisis which the patient must experience before healing can begin. Then"—listen to this—"the next day she followed the movements of a wand I held before her by moving her head back and forth."

Frau Paradies (*unimpressed*) No blood-lettings?

Herr Paradies Apparently not.

Frau Paradies Nor electrical shocks?

Herr Paradies There's no mention——

Frau Paradies They're said to be very good.

Herr Paradies They did Maria-Theresa no good.

Frau Paradies (*shrugging*) Another doctor...

Herr Paradies (*reading*) "Within another three days her trembling had completely ceased, and her health had improved enormously. At present she has a triple bandage over her eyes, as they have become very sensitive to light..." It sounds very optimistic.

Frau Paradies Does he mention our visiting her?

Herr Paradies (*scanning the letter*) "I feel, at present, that it is inadvisable for her to have visitors, as the excitement could prove extremely harmful."

Frau Paradies (*tight-lipped*) The treatment's not working.

Herr Paradies How can you——?

Frau Paradies That's why he doesn't want us to see her. After all, we're her parents. How could our presence possibly harm her? And if he's not curing her, then what *is* he up to, that's what I'd like to know?

Herr Paradies Oh, go and plump a few cushions, and stop——

Frau Paradies I've heard a few disturbing things about that man from Frau Schwartz.

She sweeps out

The Lights dim, and come up on Mesmer's house. Maria, wearing bandages over her eyes, sits playing the piano softly. She is very relaxed

Mesmer enters silently, and stands by the door. He wears a long grey robe, decorated at the hem and neck with gold lace. In his hand he carries a black wooden wand

Maria stops playing, briefly, sensing his presence, then continues

Maria (*smiling*) I know you're there, Doctor.
Mesmer You heard me?
Maria No. (*She pauses*) So much is happening all at the same time. Distractions... the light... the kindness of your wife and yourself. And, since that terrible nose-bleed, I've been able to smell things again... after all these years. Flowers... I can't wait to see their colours. And the smell of food being cooked... and perfumes... even the smell of clothes is exciting. Oh, it's like a new world! (*She pauses*) I didn't hear you, because I don't seem to listen as I did before. My mind is in such a turmoil.
Mesmer Then how did you know I was here?

Pause

Maria I don't know. (*She pauses*) Besides, I was preoccupied, thinking of Papa. This is the only time I've ever been away from him and Mama at the same time. (*During the ensuing scene she continues to play the piano*)
Mesmer You miss them?
Maria Of course.
Mesmer Would you like them to visit you?
Maria (*too quickly*) No! (*She pauses*) At least, not yet. Wait until I can see them. (*She pauses*) I wonder what they look like? (*After a pause; laughing*) He says she's a freak, and ought to be in a fairground. She says she thought she was marrying a prince, but found out he was only a frog, after all. (*She pauses*) Did I tell you she throws things? Not at me. She throws them at Papa. Once I entered a room unexpectedly, and something hit me. It fell to the floor, and I heard it break. (*She pauses*) I was very frightened. She was, too, I think. She screamed and wept and blamed Papa—but it wasn't his fault. At least... I suppose he must have provoked her... (*She pauses. She is becoming tense*) I screamed... and he slapped her. She threatened to go away, taking me with her. My back hurt, and I didn't want to go... (*She pauses*) Then I think I had one of my fits, because next thing I knew, everything seemed to be all right, and... (*She stops playing*)
Mesmer (*gently, but firmly*) Stop it. Look how you're beginning to tremble.

Pause. She begins to play again

Maria Sorry, Doctor. (*She pauses, then, brightly*) Is this a professional visit, or did you come to hear me play?
Mesmer Both. But work first. So far, you've only reacted to light through the bandages. And, although I've taken away two, I've never actually removed the third. Well, I think we're now ready for that, Fräulein.

She stops playing

Maria The light hurts my eyes...
Mesmer I know. But you must learn to accustom yourself to it. We'll just leave the bandages off for a short while to begin with. Then for longer and longer... (*He places himself behind her and begins removing the bandages*)

Act I

When they're removed, keep your eyes closed until I tell you to open them. And when you do, concentrate only on what I tell you to. Don't be too ambitious. It'll hurt, to begin with . . . (*He removes the final bandage*) Keep them closed. (*He searches around for something to show her, and selects a sheet of music, which he holds a few inches from her face*) Now. Slowly open them.

She slowly opens her eyes, and calls out in pain as she covers them with her hand, and turns her head away

Fool! Sorry, Fräulein. I should have chosen something less dazzling!

He looks around, and chooses a book with a dark cover, which he holds before her. She keeps her hands over her eyes, and her head turned away

(*Gently*) Please. Slowly open your eyes.

She turns toward the book, her hands over her eyes. Reluctantly, she opens her eyes and peers through her fingers. Slowly she moves her hands from her eyes, and begins to smile

There! That's not so bad, is it?
Maria I can . . . What is it, Doctor?
Mesmer It's a book.

She slowly reaches out to touch it

The Lights dim, and come up on the coffee house. Frau Schwartz stands gossiping to Frau Paradies, who sips coffee

Frau Schwartz . . . with thick cream, strawberries, flaked almonds, and chocolate sauce. Three of them she ate, in just under half an hour. Jokingly, I asked if she was going to have another, but she said there wasn't time, she had to rush home to eat.
Frau Paradies Poor girl. She's the size of the town hall.
Frau Schwartz And roughly the same shape. I must say it, even though she is my daughter. Her husband, on the other hand, is like a broom-handle. (*She flicks a duster over the next table*) How's *your* daughter?
Frau Paradies Progressing, apparently.
Frau Schwartz "Apparently"? You've not seen her?
Frau Paradies It's not advisable, yet.
Frau Schwartz (*nodding*) I see.
Frau Paradies Do you?
Frau Schwartz Well, you know how it is, working in a shop like this . . .?
Frau Paradies Actually, I've not had the pleasure.
Frau Schwartz People gossip. Not that I believe in repeating gossip . . .
Frau Paradies I'd never have such strength of mind. They gossip about Mesmer?
Frau Schwartz (*laughing*) Jealousy, no doubt.
Frau Paradies Jealousy?
Frau Schwartz I don't want to worry you.
Frau Paradies You've already succeeded. What sort of gossip?

Frau Schwartz Well, you must agree, he's handsome, if you care for that brooding kind of face ...
Frau Paradies Sour, I'd have called it.
Frau Schwartz Really? Anyway, he, it appears, responds equally to handsome women. Not that I'm suggesting anything ...
Frau Paradies But I thought that's just what you were doing?
Frau Schwartz Merely repeating what I've heard.

Pause

Frau Paradies No! Not my Maria-Theresa!
Frau Schwartz Of course not.

Pause

Frau Paradies What does his wife think of all this?
Frau Schwartz Well, she's about ten years older than he is, and probably welcomes his attentions being distracted. You know how it is?
Frau Paradies Ten years older?
Frau Schwartz At least. She had money.
Frau Paradies That doesn't necessarily make him lecherous.
Frau Schwartz Who mentioned lechery?
Frau Paradies You didn't actually mention anything, dear. I was merely looking for something tangible in your somewhat oblique suggestions.
Frau Schwartz Not suggestions, Frau Paradies. Just repeating what my customers tell me.

Pause

It seems he has these "rest cubicles", you see. With beds in. And when any of his lady patients have fainting spells, and the like, he treats them in these "cubicles". Alone.
Frau Paradies Have any actually complained?
Frau Schwartz No. But one or two have looked rather pleased with themselves.

Pause

He does it with his eyes, so it's said.
Frau Paradies That sounds strikingly original.
Frau Schwartz Leads them to their ... carnal doom, that is.
Frau Paradies But you've never actually met one of these ... unfortunate victims?
Frau Schwartz (*shrugging*) Who knows? It's not the sort of thing that's discussed over an apple-strudel, is it?
Frau Paradies That would depend on the ecstasy of the experience, I should imagine. (*She sips her coffee*) However, you think that's why he won't let us see her? Because she's a slave to his "depraved desires"?
Frau Schwartz (*laughing*) Whatever gave you that idea? After all, she's not exactly a pretty girl, is she? That's a comforting thought.
Frau Paradies Most comforting. Of course, she takes after her father, who, as you know, looks like a frog.

Act I

Frau Schwartz On the other hand, she's young...
Frau Paradies Another comforting thought?
Frau Schwartz The rumours may be quite unfounded.
Frau Paradies If you thought that, you wouldn't be repeating them.
Frau Schwartz Though what I always say is, where there's smoke——
Frau Paradies I think I ought to just mention the matter——
Frau Schwartz To Mesmer?
Frau Paradies Nothing quite that dramatic. To my husband.
Frau Schwartz Oh, I do hope it won't cause any trouble.
Frau Paradies If it does, I feel sure you'll be the first to know of it. Before me, in all probability.

The Lights dim, and come up on Mesmer's house. It is the occasion of one of his wife's "soirées" and in the background can be heard a string quartet. Mesmer sits reading through his notes

His wife storms in, resplendently dressed

Frau Mesmer Really, Anton. We invite people along——
Mesmer You invited them. (*He continues reading his notes*) They seem adequately entertained.
Frau Mesmer You promised to play for them.
Mesmer You promised I'd play for them. Tell them I can't.
Frau Mesmer They'd consider that rude.
Mesmer Tell them the glass-harmonica needs repairing.
Frau Mesmer They know that not to be true. Willi played on it earlier.
Mesmer In which case, it probably does need repairing. He has the gentle touch of a blacksmith. However, if it is still in tune, let him play the concerto.
Frau Mesmer He doesn't know it.
Mesmer Then tell them I've collapsed, or broken an arm, or run off with an actress. Anything. At the moment I'm busy.
Frau Mesmer You seem to find increasingly less time for me these days. Since you started treating Maria-Theresa you've——
Mesmer Less time for your so-called "soirées". I told you I didn't want the house filled with people while she's here, lest it disturb her.
Frau Mesmer We'd committed ourselves to it before you decided to accept the girl.
Mesmer It should have been cancelled.
Frau Mesmer Never! We have few enough of them these days, and I——
Mesmer Don't you realize how important it is for me to succeed in this case? Barth, Stoerck, Ingenhousz—the entire medical faculty—all of them sitting back like giant black spiders waiting for me to fail, so that they can come in for the kill. But I'm going to succeed—am succeeding—and I intend to take them up on their promise and present Maria-Theresa at Court, to prove myself. Isn't that more important than any of your frivolous evenings?
Frau Mesmer To you, it obviously is. Yet there was a time you enjoyed— even participated in—my "frivolous evenings".

Mesmer (*surprised*) It's not important to you that I prove myself?
Frau Mesmer To the medical faculty? You frequently describe them as "cretins"—so I fail to see why their good opinion should impress you. If, on the other hand, you feel the need to prove yourself to me, it's not necessary. After nine years of hard labour—or marriage, whichever term you prefer—you've already proved that what you really wanted was not a wife, but a nurse, secretary, servant, general drudge——
Mesmer You exaggerate, as usual.
Frau Mesmer —apothecary's assistant, housekeeper, special cook——
Mesmer (*wryly*) But never able to master the glass-harmonica. Are you trying to tell me you're unhappy?
Frau Mesmer (*with a false laugh*) Unhappy? Me? When did you last see anyone bursting with such good spirits? (*She turns to go, then stops*) It won't do, Anton. (*She faces him*) No ultimatum. A simple statement of fact. Either you stop taking from this marriage all the time, or I stop giving.

She goes

He watches her exit, then returns to his notes

The Lights dim, and come up on the Paradies house. Herr Paradies sits drinking coffee while his wife tries on various hats

Frau Paradies What about this one?
Herr Paradies (*not looking up*) What about it?
Frau Paradies It's not too ... too ...?
Herr Paradies (*a quick glance*) It's "too" everything; but, if it makes you happy ...
Frau Paradies Maria-Theresa will actually be able to see it.
Herr Paradies (*picking up a book and commencing reading*) It might amuse her.
Frau Paradies "Amuse her"? I'm not a circus horse.
Herr Paradies If you say so, dear.

She tries another

Frau Paradies Is this better?
Herr Paradies Better than what?
Frau Paradies Aren't you interested in what I wear?
Herr Paradies Not in the least.
Frau Paradies Most men——
Herr Paradies The coffee's cold.
Frau Paradies Mesmer said we're not to stay very long.
Herr Paradies I hate cold coffee.

The Lights dim and come up on Mesmer and Maria-Theresa. She no longer wears the bandages, and the room is still half-lit. Mesmer begins arranging a few objects to show to her. She looks at him and begins giggling

Mesmer What is it?
Maria Noses. They're so funny. I had no idea ... (*Fresh bout of giggling*)

Act I

Mesmer All noses?

She nods

What's so funny about them?
Maria The way they stick out on faces ...
Mesmer We'd look even funnier without them.
Maria That's not true. Then faces would be round, and smooth ... (*She tries to control herself*) I won't look at it.
Mesmer Try to think of something else.
Maria I'm trying.
Mesmer Think of the stars you saw last night.

Pause. She finally stops giggling

Maria They were the most beautiful thing I've seen.
Mesmer More beautiful than pictures, and trees, and animals, and——?
Maria More beautiful than anything.

He holds up a handkerchief

Mesmer What's this?

She tries hard to remember

Maria A ... a book!
Mesmer (*holding up a book*) No, Fräulein. This is a book. (*He places the handkerchief on her lap*) Now. What is it?

She closes her eyes and feels it

Maria (*smiling*) A handkerchief.

He takes it from her and holds it up

Mesmer Remember what it looks like.
Maria If I could just feel the things ...
Mesmer We both know you can recognize them by touch. Now you must learn to recognize by sight. (*He holds up a wine-glass*) What is this?
Maria It's a ... Wait a moment ... we've had this one before. It's a ... (*She is slightly agitated*) I'm such a fool, Doctor. I know I should remember, but ...
Mesmer Can you not imagine how it would feel if you were holding it?
Maria No.
Mesmer Have you tried?
Maria It looks flat. I don't know what its shape really is. (*Suddenly*) A wine-glass! It's a wine-glass!
Mesmer You see? You remembered. (*He holds up a vase*) And this?
Maria (*without hesitation*) A plate!

He demonstrates the top of the vase, indicating that it is hollow

Mesmer Try again.

She concentrates very hard, and mimes the outline of the vase

Maria This is a new one.
Mesmer You saw this one yesterday.
Maria (*distressed*) I'm so stupid.
Mesmer This is more difficult.
Maria Why?
Mesmer Because it is not quite the same one as yesterday.
Maria (*mystified*) Not quite the same one . . .? (*After a pause*) Are they not all the same shape . . . these things?
Mesmer They have one thing in common. (*He mimes picking flowers and placing them in the vase*)
Maria It's a vase!
Mesmer That's right, Fräulein. It's a vase.
Maria How can I ever remember? It's bad enough with things that are always the same shape. But when the same things can look so different . . . I can't go through life waiting for people to poke their hands inside vases before I am able to tell it's a vase.
Mesmer That's perfectly true. And that is the reason it's so necessary that you remember the names of these objects. When the medical faculty comes to see you——
Maria (*panicking*) They're coming to see me? When?
Mesmer As soon as I feel you're ready for them.
Maria But not yet. I'm not ready yet. Apart from you and your wife . . . people terrify me. Even Mama and Papa. I dread their visit, but it can't be put off any longer . . . can it?
Mesmer You promised them this afternoon, so this afternoon it must be.
Maria (*convincing herself*) It'll be all right, once they're here. I'm sure of that. It's just the thought of their coming . . .
Mesmer Everything will be fine. You'll see. And now, what have we this time?
Maria (*her hands over her eyes*) It's made my eyes very tired.

Pause

Mesmer Very well. We'll rest for a while. Play something for me.

She goes to the piano and begins playing

The Lights remain up on the scene. The Lights also come up on the Paradies house where Frau Paradies is still trying on hats, while her husband reads

Frau Paradies I do hope there's nothing going on. Frau Schwartz made me worry——
Herr Paradies You told me.
Frau Paradies (*trying on a hat*) Your reaction, to put it mildly, was hardly that of an anxious father.
Herr Paradies I refuse to work myself into a frenzy over that wretched woman's gossip.
Frau Paradies Where there's smoke——
Herr Paradies There's not necessarily an *auto-da-fé*.
Frau Paradies Apparently, there's a certain countess who says she wouldn't

Act I

be able to carry on, were it not for her regular fits of the vapours, and visits to the rest-cubicles.
Herr Paradies You've met her?
Frau Paradies Not exactly.
Herr Paradies How "exactly"?
Frau Paradies Frau Schwartz——
Herr Paradies Say no more.

She shows him another hat

Frau Paradies What about this one?
Herr Paradies (*after a brief glance*) Far too young. Were you half your age——
Frau Paradies I could be, given a little encouragement.

Maria is having difficulty with her playing. She executes a run very badly, tries it again, equally badly, and stops

Maria (*desperately*) It's no good. I've lost my touch, Doctor.
Mesmer It will return.
Maria (*shaking her head*) Simple things... that I've played a hundred times perfectly... Even when I close my eyes, pretending I'm still blind——
Mesmer (*sharply*) Don't ever do that!
Maria But it's only to help——
Mesmer (*angrily*) Learn to play with your eyes open. That's how you have to live now. Do you think I've spent all this time on you just so that you can play childish games, such as pretending that you're blind?
Maria I merely——
Mesmer Play, Fräulein. With your eyes open!

Maria begins playing

Frau Paradies has reached the last of the hats

Frau Paradies This is the last.
Herr Paradies Good.
Frau Paradies Well?
Herr Paradies (*looking up and laughing*) It's quite ridiculous. Wear it.

She hurls the hat across the room

Frau Paradies You don't care about anything, do you? What I wear, your daughter's reputation, what people say...? You just sit there, your nose in a book——
Herr Paradies Which I'd be able to read, if only you'd stop your infernal chatter!
Frau Paradies Indulging yourself, whilst our poor little girl——
Herr Paradies Our "poor little girl" appears to be perfectly well, if we're to believe Mesmer's letter, and——
Frau Paradies *If* we're to believe the letter. It's my opinion——
Herr Paradies "Your opinion"? You haven't had a personal opinion during our entire married life. What you mean is, Frau Schwartz's opinion, and I

wouldn't want her opinion even on how to make apple-strudel. Anyway, we're seeing Maria this afternoon, so we'll be able to judge for ourselves. (*He closes his book, gets up, and moves toward the door*)

Frau Paradies Where are you going?

Herr Paradies Somewhere quiet. Where I shall lock myself away, and read page after page after page. Indulgently, and quite uninterrupted!

He goes

Frau Paradies picks up a sweet dish and is about to throw it, but changes her mind, pops a sweet into her mouth and picks up the hats. The Lights dim on this area, but remain on Maria and Mesmer. Maria dejectedly stops playing

Maria Couldn't we put off their visit until tomorrow?

Mesmer And then the next day, and the next day . . .?

Maria Yesterday I felt fine. Maybe, tomorrow . . .?

Mesmer You promised them. Rest a little before they arrive.

Pause

Maria I lie there, but I don't sleep. I should be very happy . . . but I'm not. Oh, it's not your fault, Doctor.

Mesmer Nor yours. It's been very hard work—for both of us—and, well, you're tired, both in body and spirit . . . yet your mind is very active . . . grasping the situation . . .

Maria And now my music is suffering . . . the most important thing in my life.

Mesmer That's only temporary.

Pause

Maria I know it sounds ungrateful, Doctor . . . but sometimes I feel I was happier . . . as I was.

The Lights dim

CURTAIN

ACT II

The coffee house. Stoerck and Barth sit drinking coffee. Frau Schwartz hovers in the background

Stoerck ... his claims are quite ... extravagant. But that's Mesmer's style, isn't it?
Barth She can actually see?
Stoerck Apparently.
Barth Corroborated?
Stoerck Rumour. Rumour also has it that the parents are due to visit her today.
Barth Reliable rumour?
Stoerck (*nodding in the direction of Frau Schwartz*) Hell-mouth.

Frau Schwartz bustles across, smiling

Frau Schwartz You called, Herr Doctor?
Stoerck In a manner of speaking, yes. More coffee, Barth?
Barth Not for me.
Stoerck Then just one.

She bustles off

I've no doubt we'll be called to witness his tiny miracle, in the—alas—all too immediate future!
Barth If it's true, he'll be insufferable.
Stoerck When was he ever otherwise? Moreover, he'll be insistent on having the girl presented at Court.
Barth You did promise ...
Stoerck Of course I did. To be rid of him. Besides, I thought the case hopeless.
Barth We both did.
Stoerck Furthermore, at present the Empress is so thoroughly involved in totally irrelevant political intrigues that I'd probably be banished into exile—if not actually beheaded—were I to subject her to a bout of self-adulation from the modest doctor.
Barth Then how will you circumvent him?
Stoerck There must be a strategy.
Barth Reason?
Stoerck That's the least likely to succeed.

Frau Schwartz enters with his coffee

Frau Schwartz It's wonderful news about Fräulein Paradies, isn't it?
Barth Indeed. If it's true.

Frau Schwartz Oh, it's certainly true. Her mother frequently comes in here. And Frau Mesmer.
Barth Together?
Frau Schwartz No. Funnily enough, they've never met. But I discreetly talk to them both, and there's no doubt about it. The girl can see. Poor little thing. After all those years in the dark. No wonder she's so fond of the Herr Doctor.
Stoerck Is she so fond of him?
Frau Schwartz My son-in-law—drunken wastrel—took some pastries to the house, and he said that the girl watched the Herr Doctor for the entire time he was there. Watched his every move. He thought it very odd.
Stoerck Really? He said that, did he?
Frau Schwartz Well, he didn't actually say it. Even when sober, he's not exactly literate. His mother died in the mad-house, you know? No, he didn't actually say he thought it, but his manner implied it. Not that I——
Barth She could definitely see?
Frau Schwartz No doubt about it. In fact, she looked at my son-in-law and giggled. It was his nose, she said. She found it very funny. Admittedly, it is a rather unusual colour . . .

A crash of china is heard

That'll be him.

She exits hurriedly

Barth Well, Anton, I think it's time you began to think of an excuse for not presenting Mesmer and his protégée at Court.
Stoerck Or developing a hobby to while away my hours in exile . . .

They laugh

The Lights dim and come up on Mesmer's house. Maria is highly nervous as Mesmer holds various objects before her to distinguish

Mesmer (*briskly*) Come along, Fräulein. The colour.
Maria I find it difficult to——
Mesmer Concentrate!
Maria (*hesitantly*) Blue?
Mesmer Try again.
Maria Green?
Mesmer You got it right a few moments ago.
Maria (*guessing*) Yellow!
Mesmer Yellow it is. And now——

Frau Mesmer enters

Frau Mesmer Maria-Theresa's parents are here.

Maria-Theresa instinctively moves a pace closer to Mesmer

Maria You won't leave me alone with them, will you?
Mesmer Don't be foolish. They will expect——

Act II

Maria You know how strangers frighten me.
Frau Mesmer But they're not strangers——
Maria And make them go soon. Please?
Mesmer Show them in.

Frau Mesmer goes

Maria moves a little closer to Mesmer

Maria Just a little while ... as it's the first visit ...?

Her parents enter, followed by Frau Mesmer. Frau Paradies wears a huge hat

Frau Paradies Good-afternoon, Doctor.

She pauses, then sweeps across and embraces Maria, who remains rigid

Let me look at you. You look wonderful. (*To her husband*) Doesn't she look wonderful?
Maria (*listlessly*) Hallo Mama ... Papa ...
Frau Paradies A new person.

Herr Paradies moves across and kisses her. She begins to giggle

Herr Paradies (*surprised*) What is it?

She continues to giggle

Maria-Theresa!
Maria You don't ... look like ... like ... a frog! (*She continues to giggle*)
Herr Paradies A frog?
Maria Mama always said ... you looked like ... a frog. I asked the doctor to show me one ... out there ... in the garden ... and I saw ...
Frau Paradies I'm sure I——
Maria And you don't. Not a frog. But your nose ... it's ... (*She continues giggling*)
Mesmer She finds noses extremely funny.
Herr Paradies All noses?
Frau Mesmer All noses. Long, short, flat, pointed ... a constant source of amusement. You'd like some coffee, I feel sure. I'll make some.

She hurriedly exits

Maria moves away from her parents and sits on the piano stool

Mesmer Please sit down.

They seat themselves. An awkward pause

Frau Paradies This is hardly the reception we'd expected.
Mesmer What kind of a reception had you in mind, Frau Paradies? A theatrical performance?
Frau Paradies We expected her, at least, to appear pleased to see us.

Pause

Maria (*unconvincingly*) Of course I'm pleased to see you. I'm just not yet ready to meet . . . people.
Herr Paradies "People"? We're your parents, child.
Frau Paradies Or have you managed to completely forget us in two months?
Mesmer Please try to understand——
Herr Paradies I am trying to understand. So is my wife. But this . . . unfeeling attitude——
Frau Paradies After all those years we spent looking after her——
Mesmer Your daughter appreciates all that you've done for her—as much as you, yourselves, seem to appreciate it, in fact—and will continue to do so in the future, I feel sure. It's simply that, at the moment, she is still very nervous. That she can now see doesn't mean that she is completely cured. (*Softly, to Maria-Theresa*) I'll leave you alone for a while. Tell your parents all that you've been doing, Fräulein. Recognizing things . . . learning to acknowledge their shapes . . . I'll be back soon. (*To her parents*) Excuse me.

He goes

Maria panics, and appears as if about to follow him, but settles again on the piano stool. Pause

Maria (*without enthusiasm*) Well, there were exercises . . . and I had to learn to identify things that I knew only by touch . . . and . . . and . . .

Pause

Herr Paradies We've missed you.

Pause

Maria . . . and he showed me the stars. I think I liked them most of all.

Pause

Frau Paradies We so looked forward to coming here today.
Herr Paradies She spent hours selecting the hat.
Frau Paradies I wanted to look nice. Do you like it?
Maria (*vaguely*) It's very pretty.

Pause

Before you came, I was learning colours.

Pause

Frau Paradies (*impatiently*) Whatever's wrong with you, child? You can hardly bear to even speak to us. Is this why the doctor hasn't asked us to come before? Because you didn't want us here? If so, just tell us and we'll go away.
Maria (*close to tears*) I don't know why I . . . (*She shrugs miserably and stares at the keyboard*)
Frau Paradies We were perfectly acceptable while you were handicapped, and needed someone to do everything for——

Act II

Herr Paradies Stop it!
Frau Paradies Oh, it doesn't matter to you. But, then, you've never had the love and affection——
Herr Paradies I've never been ridiculous about it.
Frau Paradies Ridiculous? So you think I'm ridiculous, do you? Just because I——
Herr Paradies Quite ridiculous. I've always thought so. The doctor's already explained that Maria-Theresa's not thoroughly cured.
Frau Paradies An excuse to keep her here.
Herr Paradies Why should he do that? I'm sure his time's extremely valuable, and——
Frau Paradies (*to Maria*) Why don't you answer?
Maria What ... I ... What can I say? Perhaps, next time you come ...
Frau Paradies Will there be a next time? Who's to say——
Herr Paradies In his note, when he invited us along, he asked us not to upset her.
Frau Paradies Upset her? What about me? Doesn't it matter that I'm upset? No, I suppose not. I'm only her mother, who's devoted her life——
Herr Paradies To fussing, and shouting like a fishwife!
Frau Paradies Oh, so I'm not only ridiculous, but I'm a fishwife, too. If you've such a poor opinion of me I'm surprised you've not left me before now.
Herr Paradies The right opportunity's not arisen. Nothing quite tempting enough. But I'm not without hope.
Frau Paradies Huh! Who else would want you? You look like a frog. At least Maria-Theresa and I agree on that.

Maria begins giggling again, though this time it is more hysteria than amusement

Even Frau Schwartz's fat, spotty daughter wasn't interested enough to run away with you.
Maria A frog ...

She continues giggling, but they are now quite oblivious to her, their own conversation being of more concern

Frau Paradies Oh, don't think I was unaware of that ... horrific liaison!
Herr Paradies We merely passed the time of day——
Frau Paradies I'm fully aware of how you passed the time of day. And where. If you were about to tell me a few disgusting details, Frau Schwartz has had a rather *risqué* version circulating for months. After all, it does concern that revolting daughter of hers.
Herr Paradies Clara's a married woman.
Frau Paradies A desperate woman. Married to a man who hasn't been sober since the wedding. But, then, who can blame him?
Herr Paradies With Frau Schwartz as a mother-in-law——
Frau Paradies Married to that spotted lump, he's far better off oblivious.
Herr Paradies Clara's a lively and intelligent girl, which is more than can be said——

Frau Paradies Gross and deformed. I've never dared to ask what causes the spots. Something unspeakable, I'll be bound.
Herr Paradies I'm surprised you didn't ask her mother.

Maria, still giggling softly, has started to sway from side to side

Frau Paradies However, gross and disfigured as she is, there were times I almost wished she'd lure you away to some private hell, where you could live together in misery for ever and ever, amen. There was also an occasion I hoped you'd run off with that girl from the opera. The one with the long neck and bad breath. She seemed——

Maria suddenly screams, then sits trembling violently. Her father rushes over, and tries to embrace her, but she shrugs him away, still trembling

Herr Paradies Now see what's happened!
Frau Paradies What have we done?

She rushes over and is about to place her arm about her daughter's shoulders, but Maria cowers and moves away

Mesmer hurries in

Maria goes to him

Mesmer What have you done to her?
Frau Paradies The question is, what have *you* done to her?
Mesmer I told you she wasn't to be upset.

Frau Mesmer enters, and puts her arm about the girl

Frau Paradies She's in a worse state than when she came here. At least she used to speak to us.
Mesmer She needs time . . .
Frau Paradies Time? For what? How much time before she's ready to murder us in our beds?
Frau Mesmer I'll get her a warm drink. (*She is about to lead Maria off*)
Frau Paradies Leave her where she is. She's our daughter.
Frau Mesmer (*quietly*) You've more damage to inflict upon her?

A slight pause

Frau Mesmer leads Maria off

Frau Paradies I'm not satisfied with her condition. (*To her husband*) Are you?
Herr Paradies The doctor says she needs more time——
Frau Paradies If the doctor said she was a pickled herring, you'd believe him, I suppose?
Mesmer I fail to see the point of your remark, Frau Paradies, though you, no doubt, consider it significant. However, if that is really all you have to say, then I'll get my wife to see you out. I'm a very busy man.
Frau Paradies What about our daughter?
Mesmer She stays here.

Act II

Frau Paradies I don't think I want her to.
Herr Paradies Don't you think we ought to discuss that? Between ourselves?
Mesmer Perhaps you could discuss it elsewhere.
Frau Paradies I don't like what he's doing to her.
Mesmer I've done no more, nor less, than you asked. You wanted her to see. I've made her see.
Frau Paradies Her attitude to us is——
Mesmer I didn't promise to make her love you.

Pause

> In fact, it's of no interest to me whatsoever whether she loves you or not. My only concern lies in improving her sight, now that she has it. If *you* want that, too, then you'll not upset her, you'll not visit her until she asks for you, and, above all, you'll leave her here with me until such time as I feel she's ready to face you and live with you.

Frau Paradies And if we don't agree to these ... conditions?
Mesmer I'll get my wife to pack her clothes, and she can leave with you, today. This minute.
Herr Paradies If she comes with us, what about her sight?

Pause

Mesmer It will no longer be my concern.

Pause

Frau Paradies (*hopefully*) Once she became accustomed to being at home again, and planning recitals——
Mesmer There would be no recitals for a while.
Herr Paradies She can still play, can't she?
Mesmer Not as well as she could.
Frau Paradies Will she improve? Get back to where she was?
Mesmer (*shrugging*) Probably.
Frau Paradies You're not certain?
Mesmer I'm not a music teacher, but a doctor. And her health is of more interest to me than her musical dexterity.
Frau Paradies But she studied for all those years, and was becoming very popular——
Mesmer As a blind pianist. A kind of freak. Every playbill stressed her blindness. Her playing was good, but not exceptional. A large part of her attraction lay in the fact that she was unable to see.

Pause

> If her success as a concert pianist, and the money that it earns for her, is of more importance than the girl's sight, then I don't understand why you brought her to me. Surely you understood, right from the beginning, that with her sight she will cease to be a curiosity?

Frau Paradies (*unconvincingly*) Well, of course, her happiness is all that really matters ...

Mesmer Good. Having agreed on that, do we also agree that she stays to continue treatment?
Frau Paradies Should we not ask her?
Mesmer (*sharply*) No!

Pause

My wife has, by now, I imagine, calmed her down. I'm not prepared to have her upset again.

Pause

Later I will ask her if she wants to stay. Should she say no, you will be informed, and may come and take her home.

Pause

Herr Paradies Well, if you think it best that she remain . . .
Mesmer I do. (*He rings the bell*) I'll get my wife to see you out.

The Lights dim and come up on the coffee house. Barth sits alone. Frau Schwartz fetches his coffee

Frau Schwartz Alone today, I see.
Barth Doctor Stoerck has an appointment.
Frau Schwartz Not with Herr Paradies? I'm sorry, Professor. I shouldn't have asked. It's none of my business.
Barth (*curiously*) Why Herr Paradies?
Frau Schwartz Frau Paradies was in here yesterday, and said her husband was going to insist on seeing Doctor Stoerck, or even the Empress, if needs be. Like a madwoman she was. Even forgot to pay when she left. Not that she's to be blamed. (*After a pause, confidentially*) He won't let her go, you know.
Barth Who won't let who go?
Frau Schwartz Mesmer. He's keeping Maria-Theresa against her parents' wishes.
Barth And what of Maria-Theresa's wishes?
Frau Schwartz He seems to have some evil power over her. First of all, it seems she won't let them near her. Treats them as if they were complete strangers. Secondly, she seemed to prefer Mesmer to her own father. Ran to him, she did. Away from her parents. It's not surprising that Frau Paradies——
Barth When did they see her?
Frau Schwartz Must have been two days ago.
Barth It's true that she can see, though?
Frau Schwartz Oh, yes. And they were thankful for that. But she still has fits. Had one while they were there. Screaming, and throwing herself about. And another thing. She can't play the piano any more. That seemed to upset them—particularly Frau Paradies—more than anything. She used to play like an angel, too.
Barth She's completely forgotten?
Frau Schwartz Can't play a note. That must be very distressing for the

Act II

unfortunate girl. I mean, what's she going to do for a livelihood when she gets away from Mesmer? It's a great worry for Frau Paradies. Such a promising career she had, too. Used to travel all over Europe. (*She pauses*) Apparently, Herr Paradies wants Doctor Stoerck to make some enquiries regarding the sort of treatment his daughter is having. He talks of "dangerous experiments" going on in Mesmer's laboratory. Though what he means by that, I've no idea. I don't think Herr Paradies does, either. In my opinion, he's been listening to a lot of idle gossip. And you know how gossip-mongers exaggerate things. (*She pauses*) Then, of course, there are those who think he's dabbling in magic. I mean, that's not the sort of thing you expect from a doctor, is it?

Barth Well, his methods——

Frau Schwartz I shudder to think of it. (*Confidentially*) They do say, however, that there are those who want the Empress to set up one of her Court Commissions to investigate his activities.

Barth You seem remarkably well-informed, Frau Schwartz. You didn't happen to hear who "those" were?

Frau Schwartz (*shrugging*) It could be jealousy. They say that, too. And, if it's jealousy, then, obviously, it would have to be the doctors and the medical faculty, and ... Oh, I'm sorry, professor, I——

Barth But it's merely gossip, which you, yourself, don't believe for one minute—as I'm sure you were about to add.

Frau Schwartz (*with a weak smile*) You read my mind, Professor.

Pause

I can tell you one thing, though. Were she my daughter, I'd get her away from there before she became one of his accolades.

Barth "Acolytes", I think.

Frau Schwartz Well, at least we agree on it.

Barth (*raising his eyebrows*) Do we?

The Lights dim and come up on the Paradies house. Herr Paradies stands staring out of the window. His wife sits listlessly huddled in a chair

Frau Paradies You didn't see Stoerck, then?

Herr Paradies How many times do you need to be told?

Frau Paradies You, who were so absolutely determined.

Herr Paradies He was away, attending a patient.

Frau Paradies You should have waited. But no, it gave you the opportunity to put it off for another day.

Herr Paradies If you're so insistent on having her back, go to Mesmer and tell him. He said she can come with us.

Frau Paradies Against her will? That'll make for a very happy household, won't it?

Herr Paradies Even should Stoerck order him to let her go, it would still be against her will.

Frau Paradies At least the onus of responsibility would be on him. She couldn't blame us. Not that she would directly blame us, anyway. I doubt she'd even open her mouth, or stay in the same room with us, once she

were home. To start with, at least.
Herr Paradies Then leave her where she is, for the time being.
Frau Paradies I really do not understand how you can remain so totally . . . non-committal . . . about the wretched business. The way she ignored us, and ran to that . . . creature . . . as though . . . as though . . .
Herr Paradies "As though" what?
Frau Paradies I really don't know.
Herr Paradies As though he were her father?

Pause

That, apparently, is how you described it to that witch at the coffee house.

Pause

Frau Paradies Or worse.

Pause

Herr Paradies Is it your intention to provoke a scandal?
Frau Paradies You think it impossible that anyone should find her attractive?
Herr Paradies Merely improbable. Besides, his wife's always present.
Frau Paradies Not always.
Herr Paradies To me, the relationship appeared quite formal.
Frau Paradies Not to me.
Herr Paradies Your instinct at work?
Frau Paradies Were you a little more sensitive regarding your daughter——
Herr Paradies Were you a little less sensitive, you'd trust her.
Frau Paradies It's him I don't trust. After all, she's only eighteen, and he's in his forties. As for that wife of his, she must be fifty-five, if she's a day. Doesn't that make the idea at least . . . feasible?
Herr Paradies Even were he the essence of lechery incarnate——
Frau Paradies Ah, so you're willing to concede——
Herr Paradies It wouldn't necessarily follow that Maria-Theresa was the object of a grand passion. The idea is too ridiculous. She has no more the attributes for exciting a grand passion than you. She's dull, like all the women in your family. And, like all the women in your family, probably cold and unresponsive, too. Anyway, assuming he were absolutely desperate, and turned to her for comfort, how would you prove the relationship?
Frau Paradies Ask her. She's always been a truthful child.
Herr Paradies You think she'd admit to it?

Pause

Frau Paradies There are always medical tests.
Herr Paradies And if it were proved that the evil was all in your fertile imagination?
Frau Paradies At least we'd know.
Herr Paradies That would be a great consolation, as we sat in our respective cells, counting off the years, wouldn't it? For Mesmer would certainly not

Act II

let the slander rest there. He couldn't. His reputation as a doctor——
Frau Paradies That couldn't suffer any more harm.
Herr Paradies Nevertheless, he'd be obliged to make an issue of the matter. As for Maria-Theresa, do you think we'd ever repair the damage done? Having distrusted her, and made a public spectacle of her, do you think she'd return to us brimming with filial love and affection?
Frau Paradies Why do you completely nullify every single utterance I make?
Herr Paradies To prevent us living in a world of unparalleled fantasy.
Frau Paradies You saw for yourself how she preferred him to us. That wasn't fantasy. Nor is the fact he's ruined her as a musician.
Herr Paradies It's probably only temporary.
Frau Paradies "Probably". That's what he said. What if it's permanent? What if she doesn't ever play again?
Herr Paradies We'll find something else for her.
Frau Paradies Something to compensate for what she'll lose on concerts? Don't forget, the Empress's bursary will stop. It's paid to help with her music lessons. If she has no lessons ... ergo, no bursary.

Pause

Herr Paradies I thought it was her sight that we were really concerned about.
Frau Paradies That *you* were concerned about. Maria-Theresa has never expressed any desire to see. Her music was all that mattered to her. Anyway, we're not even sure she can see.
Herr Paradies However little, it's an improvement.
Frau Paradies I had expectations of her reading scores ... improving her technique ... furthering her repertoire, and career ... Yet how does she employ whatever sight she has? She goes into hysterics at the very sight of a nose. And your nose, at that. Had she any feelings she'd have pretended not to notice the wretched thing.
Herr Paradies It's not classical, I agree——
Frau Paradies We both agree. And thank heavens for that. One needs elegance and height to carry off a classical nose. Giggling like some poor mad thing. I could have wept. That girl's in a worse state than when she went to that charlatan.
Herr Paradies She simply needs more time. He said she's not quite——
Frau Paradies Oh, what's the good of talking to you about it? You just don't understand how a mother feels.

She storms out

The Lights dim, and come up on the coffee house. Frau Schwartz chats to Barth

Frau Schwartz ... apparently he locked the poor girl away and told her parents to get out of his house.
Barth Did Frau Paradies actually tell you that?
Frau Schwartz Well ... not exactly.

Barth Then do you think you should be repeating it?
Frau Schwartz People never tell you everything, do they? They always keep some choice little morsel to themselves. You have to fill in the spaces. Fortunately, I know her better than she knows herself. She's been coming here for years. And her husband. He'd stay for hours talking to my Clara. Very friendly.
Barth Your Clara?
Frau Schwartz My daughter. You must have seen her. Vast, with a most unfortunate complexion. You might care to look at it some time, Professor. I'm sure it's something very interesting that she has. On second thoughts, perhaps I'd rather not know.

Pause

Is it true that you once tried to cure the Paradies girl?
Barth Yes. It seemed hopeless. We tried everything.
Frau Schwartz But you tried with . . . medical things, of course?
Barth Of course.
Frau Schwartz Ah.
Barth You believe he does it with magic?
Frau Schwartz (*shrugging*) There are those who say he's sold his soul to the devil.
Barth Then he didn't get much in return, did he? He's considered a charlatan, vilified by every gossip in Vienna, and can't even claim success with all his patients. You'd think he'd have set a higher price on his soul, wouldn't you? (*He rises, and hands money to her*) I must go. As pleasant as it is sitting here gossiping, I've work to do.
Frau Schwartz A little relaxation does us all good. (*Enquiringly*) I hope I haven't kept you from something important?
Barth What could be more important than keeping a finger on the pulse of Vienna? (*As he goes he almost collides with . . .*)

Frau Paradies as she rushes in

Good-morning, Frau Paradies.

She turns her head, and snubs him

Barth goes

Frau Paradies (*sitting*) That man!
Frau Schwartz You don't like——
Frau Paradies He and Stoerck were responsible for sending my daughter to Mesmer.
Frau Schwartz But I thought it was your husband's idea?
Frau Paradies He's just as bad. A gullible fool.
Frau Schwartz All men are fools.
Frau Paradies I want my daughter back——
Frau Schwartz Naturally.
Frau Paradies And he says "wait", and "maybe she needs more time", and——

Act II

Frau Schwartz Mere excuses, to put off until tomorrow what they can't be bothered to do today. My husband was much the same—rest his soul—and would have put off going to his Maker, had his Maker not been so insistent. Though I sometimes wonder whether he'd made some special arrangement, and went for sheer spite, to avoid Clara's wedding. He hated weddings. For that matter, he hated Clara. Died three days before she got married. That was a busy week for me, I can tell you. But I know just how you feel. If that were my daughter, I'd storm in there and take her by force!
Frau Paradies That's just what I feel inclined to do.
Frau Schwartz After all, she can see, and that's what she went there for, isn't it?
Frau Paradies It's only that ... well, you probably know how she rejected us ... both her father and me ...
Frau Schwartz I simply don't know what's becoming of this modern generation of children.
Frau Paradies If I drag her away, what's it going to be like with her moping about her own home, wanting to be there with him ... and that wife of his, who's no better.
Frau Schwartz (*interested*) Isn't she?
Frau Paradies She was rude to me.
Frau Schwartz I can see that she could be.
Frau Paradies When I asked for Maria-Theresa back, she said, "Why? Have you some more damage to do to her?"
Frau Schwartz (*disappointed*) Very cutting.
Frau Paradies Any damage was done by that infamous pair.
Frau Schwartz I so understand your concern, Frau Paradies. Especially with rumours being as rife as they are regarding his ... behaviour ... with his female patients. Not that I'm implying——
Frau Paradies You're the very soul of discretion. What behaviour?
Frau Schwartz Well ... they say he sits facing the ladies ... with their knees touching ... and he then strokes them.
Frau Paradies Where?
Frau Schwartz In the rest-cubicles.
Frau Paradies I didn't expect him to do it in the Landstrasse. I mean, what part of their ... bodies?
Frau Schwartz Some say the face ... some the arms ... The ones who appear to really enjoy themselves just sit and look smug.
Frau Paradies What are they saying about my daughter?
Frau Schwartz (*evasively*) Well, she's an inexperienced girl, and no doubt she's flattered by the attention of the doctor ... an older man ... not understanding how such a relationship can be misconstrued by the vicious slanders circulating these days. Once upon a time conversation over a cup of coffee was an innocent, highly civilized amusement, but——
Frau Paradies What, exactly, are they saying?

Pause

Frau Schwartz Nothing ... tangible, but ... (*She shrugs*) Will you take coffee?

Frau Paradies Yes. No. (*She stands*) If my husband won't do anything about it, then I shall have to do it myself.
Frau Schwartz Oh, I do hope I haven't——
Frau Paradies Thank you for helping me to make up my mind.

She goes

Frau Schwartz smiles blissfully

The Lights dim, and come up on Mesmer's house. He sits watching as Maria-Theresa plays the piano

Maria (*delighted*) I'm very much improved, aren't I, Doctor?
Mesmer I told you you'd improve.
Maria There were times I despaired of ever playing well again.
Mesmer You didn't trust me.
Maria That's true. (*She pauses*) I should have trusted you. All the other things you promised happened. My sight ... my sense of smell ... the fits stopped. (*She pauses*) All of this must stop, too, mustn't it? This ... interlude. Soon I must go back ... home.
Mesmer Naturally. But only when your cure is complete, Fräulein.
Maria It was never home. Home should be warm, and comfortable. Like a favourite cloak.
Mesmer Things will be different. You will return to your career—and that's what you want, isn't it? With the added advantage of being able to see the beautiful cities you visit. Prague ... Paris ... Salzburg.
Maria (*smiling*) I'll also be able to see Papa—who doesn't look like a frog ... and watch Mama throw things at him ... and him slapping her ... (*She pauses*) I take the most depressing view, don't I?
Mesmer It's well that you should be prepared for these things. But you're a strong enough character to see them for what they really are. Petty domestic squabbles. Unimportant. Imagine, instead, your first public concert. The spectacle of rich silks, brocades, jewels, glittering chandeliers ... white-gloved hands applauding you. *You*, Fräulein. The journeys you'll make. The countryside in autumn ... at its most beautiful. Won't you give a little thought to these things?
Frau Paradies (*off*) I will see her!
Frau Mesmer (*off*) Are you sure it's advisable, under——?
Frau Paradies (*off*) And take her away from this——
Frau Mesmer (*off*) When you are calmer——
Frau Paradies (*off*) Get out of my way!
Frau Mesmer (*off*) This is still my house, Frau Paradies!

During this scene Maria has become very tense, and moves quickly to escape the inevitable meeting with her mother. She is about to leave the room, but stops when Mesmer speaks

Mesmer You're merely postponing the scene.
Frau Paradies (*off*) So help me, I'll strike you, if you don't——
Frau Mesmer (*off*) I'd welcome the attempt. It would give me the opportunity to retaliate.

Act II

Maria I'm sorry, Doctor. It seems I'm not a strong enough character.

She goes

Frau Paradies storms into the room, followed by Frau Mesmer

Frau Paradies Where is she?
Frau Mesmer I tried to stop her.
Mesmer I heard. I imagine the whole street did. A valiant attempt, my dear. (*To Frau Paradies*) And to what do I owe this pleasure, madam?
Frau Paradies The pleasure's entirely yours. Where is she? Locked up, no doubt!
Mesmer As a matter of fact, she was sitting here calmly playing the piano, prior to your subtle entrance.
Frau Paradies Playing the piano? But you told us that she couldn't play. More of your trickery? If she can see, and play again, why are you keeping her here?
Mesmer Because, in my opinion, she is not ready to go back to you yet.
Frau Paradies And in my opinion, she is. So I've come to take her.
Frau Mesmer But it could undo——
Frau Paradies I'm addressing your husband. He's the doctor—so we're told.
Mesmer If you'll excuse me, I'd better see how she is. My wife will entertain you. (*He goes to the door, and turns*) You'd be ill-advised to try striking Frau Mesmer. She comes from a long military line.

He goes

Frau Mesmer Look, Frau Paradies, your daughter's——
Frau Paradies "She's not ready yet . . . she's not ready yet . . ." That's all we hear from him, and it's a lie. She's perfectly——
Frau Mesmer You're quite right, Frau Paradies. It is a lie.
Frau Paradies You actually admit——
Frau Mesmer At least, part lie. Though why he should hide the truth from you is quite beyond my comprehension. The simple fact is, that she has tasted an atmosphere here so vastly different from that gory battlefield you call home, that she's absolutely terrified to return.
Frau Paradies How dare you——
Frau Mesmer And who can blame her for that? She's a sensitive, intelligent girl who is treated little better than a beast of burden. In the short time I've known her, I've learned to feel for, and understand her, to a far greater degree than you will ever experience, and——
Frau Paradies So that's it! It's you who's been turning her against us!
Frau Mesmer No. The pair of you turned her——
Frau Paradies You've turned her against her natural parents!
Frau Mesmer Natural? You're as natural as the mating between a viper and a scorpion. Had the girl not an infinite capacity for suffering she'd be in a madhouse by now.
Frau Paradies She'd be far better off with us than imprisoned here with a charlatan and a shrew. Thank heavens I decided to come here today. I

thought it was just his evil influence that was affecting her. I'd no idea of your hidden talents.
Frau Mesmer If you take her back to that atmosphere——
Frau Paradies Which is my firm intent——
Frau Mesmer You'll probably undo all of the good that's been done.
Frau Paradies Good? Huh! If you think——

Mesmer enters, bringing Maria with him. She is terrified

Maria Hallo, Mama.

Frau Paradies goes to her

Frau Paradies My poor baby. What have they been doing to you?
Maria I'm feeling quite well, Mama.
Frau Paradies You're looking very pale. Probably don't get enough to eat. You've missed Mama's cooking, haven't you? Never mind. When we get home——
Maria (*sharply*) Home?
Frau Paradies There! Isn't that a pleasant surprise? I've come to take you home. The doctor can send your clothes——
Maria (*a note of hysteria*) No!
Frau Paradies Your papa is most anxious to see you.
Maria (*shaking her head*) No. Not yet. I——
Frau Paradies (*grabbing her wrist*) Everything will be fine, once you're——
Maria (*trying to shake loose*) No! I don't want to——
Mesmer That is not——
Maria Let me go!
Frau Paradies You ungrateful wretch. You're every bit as bad as the rest of them in this house. The sooner you're away, the better!
Maria Please, Mama. Let me stay. Just for——
Frau Paradies For not another minute shall you remain here!

Maria is still struggling to escape, and her mother hurls the girl away from her. As Maria falls she hits her head. Mesmer and his wife rush to help her rise

Frau Mesmer You stupid woman.
Frau Paradies And now, if you'll pack her clothes——

She is interrupted by the moaning of the girl

Maria No . . . no . . . no . . . (*She shakes her head, and places her hands over her eyes*) I'm sorry . . . I'm sorry . . . I'm sorry . . . (*She gropes for Mesmer's hand*) So sorry, Doctor . . .
Mesmer (*looking into her eyes*) So much good work . . . wasted!

He stands and faces Frau Paradies as Frau Mesmer puts her arms around the girl

Frau Mesmer There, there, Maria . . .
Mesmer (*coldly*) You wanted your daughter back, madam. Take her. I return her to you just as I found her. Blind. (*He moves to the door*) And never let me see you again.

Act II

He goes

Frau Mesmer continues to embrace the girl

Frau Paradies I didn't mean it ... I'm sorry ... I didn't mean it ... if only I'd ... (*She reaches out and touches Maria's face*)
Maria (*savagely*) Leave me alone!

Frau Paradies withdraws her hand as though stung. She covers her face and cries

The scene dims, and the Lights come up on the Paradies house. Herr Paradies sits talking to Barth

Herr Paradies How is my wife today, Doctor?
Barth Much the same. I've given her something to quieten her. She'll sleep, and forget about it for a while.
Herr Paradies It was a great shock.
Barth (*acidly*) For your daughter too, I imagine.
Herr Paradies Oh, of course. Poor Maria. I told my wife it was a silly——
Barth Imbecile——
Herr Paradies ——thing to do. But she was very worried——
Barth Absolute imbecile. Even someone less volatile than Mesmer would have felt murderous, seeing months of work destroyed in a brief moment of senseless anger. I'm surprised he didn't throw your wife out, bodily.
Herr Paradies He wouldn't?
Barth I'd not lay a wager on that.
Herr Paradies Did he agree to see you?
Barth Most reluctantly.
Herr Paradies Did Doctor Stoerck go with you?
Barth No. The spirit was willing, but the flesh was weak. He suddenly found an urgent appointment that sent him in the opposite direction.
Herr Paradies You talked with Mesmer?
Barth Eventually. But first, I had to listen to him. At considerable length. A lecture on his beloved animal-magnetism ... followed by beratings for not having acknowledged his genius ... then on to his general discontent with the behaviour of the medical faculty, Vienna and the Viennese ... with a special little mention for Frau Schwartz ... on to descriptions of yourself and your wife which were not merely scurrilous, but quite obscene ... all the ills of the world, *ad infinitum*, until, blissfully, he became so agitated that he began to choke. I pounced, before he could recover his breath and continue his monologue.
Herr Paradies And you asked him?
Barth Yes. He said, at first, that you could go and fetch her home, he wanted nothing to do with anyone either associated with, or related to, you or your wife.

The Lights remain on this scene. A further Light goes up on Mesmer

Mesmer Furthermore, I'd as soon have the black plague in this house as either of those ingrates. Take her with you, Barth, and drop her on their doorstep, with my compliments.

Barth moves into Mesmer's area

Barth Don't you think that an unreasonable attitude?

Mesmer Were I unreasonable, you would not have been allowed in to plead for them.

Barth I'm thinking of the girl.

Mesmer Your humanitarian leanings do you credit, Barth, albeit somewhat late. It's a great pity this admirable sentiment failed to surface until the unfortunate incident occurred. Had you acknowledged the miraculous cure earlier——

Barth "Miraculous"?

Mesmer (*smiling*) Why not? It hasn't escaped my attention that I'm referred to, in some quarters, as "The Wizard". Had you acknowledged the cure, there would have been none of the slanderous gossip, and that weather-beaten hag would not have stormed in here like an avenging fury!

Barth Scandal wasn't the reason. She was worried because her daughter appeared to have lost all of her affection for her parents.

Mesmer She hadn't "lost all her affection"—it was merely in a state of suspension. She wasn't ready to go back into her cage. Given time, I'd have prepared her for that unappetizing little adventure, even, and she would have accepted it as she'd accepted all the other alterations in her life. But those fools didn't trust me any more than you.

Barth If I didn't trust you I wouldn't be here appealing for you to continue with the treatment.

Mesmer You wouldn't be here had Paradies not used a little influence at Court. You're no friend of the family. Did the Empress ask you to intervene?

Barth His wife is hysterical.

Mesmer She's in a permanent state of hysteria. It's her only distinguishing feature.

Barth Whatever the reason for my being here, the Court, or her mother's tactless visit, is it fair to penalize the girl for what happened?

Mesmer You're trying to reduce me to tears——

Barth I'm trying to awaken you to your responsibilities as a doctor.

Mesmer "Responsibilities"? "Irresponsible" is the customary epithet. As for being a doctor, I thought that was a matter for conjecture? "Magician" ... "wizard" ... "charlatan" ... Surely, these are the current opinions? Stop trying to be tactful, Barth ... or flattering ... whichever role you see yourself playing ... and consider the situation in its actuality. Someone ... be it Paradies, or a chamberlain ... or, indeed, the Empress, herself ... has entrusted you with this ... delicate mission ... and you're hoping to survive it with grace and honour. Who knows—there might even be advancement in it for you.

They stare at each other for a moment

Were I to do this for you ... for *you*, and not that cretinous pair ... would you do something for me in return?

Barth (*warily*) That would depend.

Act II

Mesmer (*smiling*) Cautious, even with your back firmly against a wall?
Barth Why not? You've frequently accused me of being conservative and conventional. Did you expect me to leap out of character with a rash, unqualified "yes"?
Mesmer I'm not that drunk on success.
Barth Success?
Mesmer In a position to make terms. I consider that an unparalleled success after the cavalier way I've been treated.
Barth What is it you want?
Mesmer If I restore the girl's sight, I want your reassurance that I shall have the opportunity to demonstrate the fact before the members of the medical faculty. And that she'll be presented to the Empress.
Barth This was already promised.
Mesmer Promises get carelessly forgotten. This time I want it in the form of a written agreement.
Barth Very well. As soon as you think her sufficiently cured——
Mesmer I will inform you. Unless, of course, Frau Schwartz gets the news to you first. My wife will see you out. (*He begins to move away, then turns*) And you can tell her parents that I never ever want to set eyes on them again. Neither in this life, nor the next, if it can be arranged.

He goes

The Light in that area dims. Barth enters the scene with Herr Paradies

Herr Paradies So he agreed to continue?
Barth I never doubted that he would. In fact, I suspect he had already started, prior to my visit.
Herr Paradies Why? After my wife's treatment of him?
Barth His consuming vanity. Where everyone else failed, he made her see. If he can do it again it will prove what idiots the rest of us are. Particularly myself. He will become revoltingly complacent.
Herr Paradies And she will be presented to the Empress?

Pause

Barth We'll see.

The Lights dim and come up on Mesmer's house. Frau Mesmer sits looking through some letters

Her husband enters, looking pre-occupied

Mesmer She's not responding quite as well this time.
Frau Mesmer Three more "we regret we are unable to attend" letters. That makes eleven.
Mesmer She's disturbed, I think, at the prospect she may lose her skill at the pianoforte again.
Frau Mesmer Even the French ambassador ...
Mesmer She's regained all her former ability. Her touch is beautiful. You must have heard her. Only yesterday, she——
Frau Mesmer Anton! Do you think we might spend an odd moment or two talking of our own—personal—affairs?

Mesmer (*coldly*) I was under the impression my work *is* our own—personal—affair?
Frau Mesmer Obviously to a differing degree.
Mesmer (*impatiently*) Very well, Anna. What do you want to talk about?
Frau Mesmer As gracious as ever. It's with regard to May the twenty-third.

Pause

Just as I suspected. You've forgotten.
Mesmer Our wedding anniversary?
Frau Mesmer That's January. Try again.
Mesmer Then it must be a birthday.
Frau Mesmer Bravo. Your forty-third. After that number of birthdays one would expect you to remember the date, if not exactly how old you are. Particularly since we discussed the guest-list for the soirée together.
Mesmer We're always having soirées. How can I be expected to remember details? One is much the same as another.
Frau Mesmer This one should prove very different. Very sparsely attended, if we continue receiving "regrets" from our invited guests at the present rate.
Mesmer There's probably a rival event. Is that all you wanted to discuss?
Frau Mesmer The reasons given are as varied as they appear to be untrue.
Mesmer Why should they——?
Frau Mesmer Isn't it time you brought your head out of the clouds for long enough to acknowledge that you are the current scandal of Vienna?
Mesmer I've always been the current scandal. There's no-one more interesting to talk about.
Frau Mesmer This isn't the usual "charlatan" gossip.
Mesmer (*tiredly*) What is it this time?
Frau Mesmer It concerns Fräulein Paradies.
Mesmer You just said they were talking about me.
Frau Mesmer Both of you. It's suggested she's your mistress.

Pause

Mesmer But she's only a child.
Frau Mesmer That only makes things worse. Were she some highly-painted doxy they might even sympathize with you. After all, we're both aware that they consider me old enough to be your mother, and a little past that sort of thing. But the idea of you and that child together seems to incense them. They even harbour dark thoughts about her being under your spell. Sorcery, no less!
Mesmer You shouldn't listen to their stupid chatter.
Frau Mesmer How can I avoid it? Everywhere I go the conversation stops as though they'd all been suddenly struck dumb. Were it not for a few spurious friends who "thought I ought to know" I'd still be wondering whether I was a suspected smallpox carrier. Even some of those we thought of as friends are obviously taking it seriously. It no longer seems considered *de rigueur* to be seen at our gatherings.
Mesmer Then cancel the accursed thing.

Act II

Frau Mesmer (*firmly*) No.
Mesmer If no-one wants to attend——
Frau Mesmer That would be capitulation.
Mesmer Ah, it brings out the old military strain in you!
Frau Mesmer For me there has always been a social life, and it means a great deal.
Mesmer Most of these glittering occasions are vulgar extravagant gestures, furnishing hostesses with the opportunity to try outshining each other!
Frau Mesmer Dear me. Am I really that shallow?
Mesmer If I had my way——
Frau Mesmer Should you have your way, dear husband, there would be no more such occasions. Ever. For either of us. I am quite aware of that. But we are being ostracized——
Mesmer If that's how they feel, forget them!
Frau Mesmer No, Anton. My soirées give me much pleasure. As for their "vulgar extravagance"——
Mesmer I know. It's your money.

Pause

Frau Mesmer Have I ever used that argument?
Mesmer Many think that's why I married you. The rich widow.
Frau Mesmer Equally, there are many who think I married you to get out of the clutches of my mother-in-law, a dragon who was, not to put too fine a point on it, thrifty. However, what I had intended to say was that these "vulgar, extravagant occasions" were your entrée into Viennese society, and you weren't so contemptuous then. Nor were you averse to moving among my friends, talking the ears off any who were unfortunate enough to be inveigled into stopping to listen.
Mesmer Most of them had little of consequence to say for themselves.
Frau Mesmer Most of them had—and have—a wide variety of interests, whereas you, on the other hand, have nothing but animal-magnetism.
Mesmer Nothing but animal-magnetism? It's a revol——
Frau Mesmer Please, Anton. I've heard it all before. Several times a day for nine years.
Mesmer I'm a bore?
Frau Mesmer A little unadventurous in conversation.
Mesmer Then in future I shall not bore you, nor your friends, since I shall not be present at any of your "soirées".
Frau Mesmer A childish, quite predictable, attitude.
Mesmer As for this birthday evening you've planned, it can easily be cancelled.
Frau Mesmer Not for the Empress's jewels!
Mesmer Say I'm indisposed.
Frau Mesmer And admit you're afraid to face them?
Mesmer Afraid? Of a handful of malicious gossips?
Frau Mesmer Giving them cause to believe the liaison to be true?
Mesmer If that's what they want to believe——

Frau Mesmer They will. And, should the Empress hear of it, she'll no doubt set up one of her tiresome commissions. On morals. Even were you proved innocent, do you think that would clear your reputation? Doubts would remain.
Mesmer My reputation will be cleared when I present the girl at Court, able to see, and in perfect health. All this other ... sewage ... about witchcraft, and immorality ... and the ostracism ... will be seen for what it is. Incredible jealousy!
Frau Mesmer I'm afraid I don't share your optimism.
Mesmer What are you suggesting that I do?

Pause

Frau Mesmer Send her back to her parents.
Mesmer Are you that intimidated by scandal?
Frau Mesmer Once she's gone, the matter will die. There'll be nothing for it to feed on.
Mesmer She's not ready yet.
Frau Mesmer It seems the longer she stays, the more difficult it becomes for her to face them. Will you still be claiming she's not ready in two or three years time?
Mesmer If necessary——
Frau Mesmer When will she ever be ready?

Pause

Mesmer I won't have my work interfered with.
Frau Mesmer And I won't have my life in ruins because——
Mesmer You exaggerate, as usual.

She offers him the letters

Frau Mesmer See for yourself.

He doesn't even glance at them

Mesmer If everyone refused to come, I'd still keep the girl until I consider her fit to leave.

He goes quickly

His wife stares at the letters

The Lights dim and come up on the Paradies house. Frau Paradies sits in a chair with a blanket over her knees. Her husband reads a letter to her, which he has just written

Herr Paradies "... and cannot thank you enough for all that you have done for our beloved daughter. Your patience and determination have filled us with admiration——"
Frau Paradies Patience! D'you think he understands the word?
Herr Paradies We must be tactful. (*He continues reading*) "... also the love and affection shown by your wife."

Act II

Frau Paradies That shrew!
Herr Paradies (*reading*) "We have heard extremely good reports of Maria's health, and that her sight is restored. I regret to tell you that my wife is not yet in the best of health, but feel sure that once our daughter is returned to us she will completely recover. Therefore, I request that you please allow her to return to us, where she will have the opportunity to recuperate in the country air. If you agree to this, I promise that she will be returned to you immediately, should it be felt necessary, in the interests of her health, to do so."
Frau Paradies Over my dead body!
Herr Paradies Were we to send the sort of letter you'd write he'd never return her to us.
Frau Paradies She'll never go back to him. Never. Once she's here it will be the last he'll ever hear of her. Five months she's been in the ... den ... of that monster. Heaven knows what sort of a state she's in now. We don't even know that she recognizes us any longer!
Herr Paradies I'll send the letter, and we'll see what happens.

The Lights dim and come up on the coffee house. Stoerck and Barth are talking

Stoerck The man's a fool. While it has been an embarrassment having him expounding highly imaginative fantasies, and ridiculing the medical faculty, that was at least a purely medical matter. But to allow himself to become the centre of a sordid scandal involving one of his patients is the act of an utter madman. It also raises suspicions with regard to others of his female patients. Husbands are beginning to suspect their wives of all manner of depravities.
Barth Do you believe the gossip?
Stoerck What does it matter what I believe? It's what Vienna believes that reflects on the faculty. And he is still a member of the faculty, alas. I wrote to him recently, telling him to put an end to this situation by returning the girl to her parents, if he thought it could be done without risk. Needless to say, there was no reply.
Barth No doubt he's still smarting at our lack of enthusiasm for the claims at the demonstration he arranged for us.
Stoerck I thought we handled the situation with immense charm and subtlety.
Barth He's not fool enough to fail to notice how completely non-committal—indeed, almost irrelevant—your remarks were.
Stoerck What did he expect? Oh, it was impressive, I grant you. Dramatic. But not conclusive. As I've always said, he should be in the theatre. You were hardly overwhelmed.
Barth Too many tricks, I thought. The point that struck me most was that she appeared to have memorized her part badly. For instance, when he held a cup before her, she said it was a sweet bowl. And thought that blue was yellow. As though he'd given her a number of things to remember, then held them up in the wrong order. As you know, I've had a great deal of experience with eye disease ... some of my patients were completely blinded with cataracts ... and I've restored their sight ... yet none ever

responded as ... haphazardly ... as that girl. As for that cabalistic robe he wore ... he looked like a fairground performer!

Stoerck The girl's father is writing to him, asking for her return.

Barth And if he refuses?

Stoerck Paradies intends demanding drastic action ... and I shudder to think of the further scandal that would involve.

The Lights dim, and come up on the Mesmer house. Maria, serene and happy, plays the piano

Mesmer enters

Maria A piece by Herr Mozart. Such talent. (*She continues playing for a moment, then looks at Mesmer. She stops playing and goes closer to look into his face*) I sensed it. You're unhappy.

Mesmer I've had a letter from your father.

Pause

Maria (*resignedly*) Asking for my return.

Mesmer If you feel unable to ...

She silences him by raising her hand. She seems about to touch his face, but desists, and returns to her seat at the piano

Maria I've thought about it a great deal lately. It's inevitable that I go, isn't it? (*She smiles, and resumes playing*) You thought I'd have one of my fits, didn't you?

Pause

I could cry. But that's not the same thing. At leaving you and your dear wife.

Pause

It's so peaceful here.

Mesmer He has promised to send you to me if ever you should need me.

Maria (*wryly*) I'm sure he has.

Pause

Will you come to hear my concerts?

Mesmer With pleasure.

Maria If they still want me, that is, now that I'm no longer "the celebrated blind pianist"!

Mesmer Of course they'll want you. You're young, with promise of immense virtuosity.

Pause

Maria Am I to go soon?

Mesmer I'll leave that decision to you.

Pause

Maria Tomorrow. Not today.

Act II

Mesmer (*nodding*) Tomorrow.

Frau Mesmer enters

Maria (*rising; close to tears*) I'll go to my room for a while.

She goes quickly

Frau Mesmer You've told her?

Mesmer Would you rather I had left the pleasure to you?

Frau Mesmer Pleasure? I thought we renounced pleasure when you became a prophet. As for the girl—of course I'm sorry to see her go back to those dreadful parents——

Mesmer But, on the other hand, it solves your problems, doesn't it?

Frau Mesmer Her departure's a little too late for that, I'm afraid. Your birthday dinner was a fiasco. As well-attended as a pauper's funeral. Those who did arrive—out of morbid curiosity, I'm convinced—are doubtless circulating wild distortions of the extent of the disaster.

Mesmer And that's all that interests you?

Frau Mesmer Had I been indifferent to the girl I would hardly have spent these months nursing her.

Mesmer (*as if she hasn't spoken*) She'll go back to that hell, and you'll go back to titillating the jaded palates of your friends as if nothing has happened.

Frau Mesmer "My" friends? A few months ago they were "our" friends. And—surprisingly enough—a few of those "jaded palates" still believe in you, despite the slanders.

Mesmer How noble of them. But why "surprisingly"?

Frau Mesmer You do little to deserve their loyalty. Even in the present circumstances you continue to flaunt your eccentricities as though they were a handful of priceless jewels. You're rude to them if they refuse to listen to your endless dissertations, and arrogantly condescending if they do. Is it your intention to alienate the few friends we have left? Isn't the scorn of the medical faculty, and the malice of three-quarters of Vienna sufficient to satisfy you? Must it be everyone? As a sign of the world's crass stupidity?

Mesmer I don't need your so-called friends. And I've no intention of standing mute just to "deserve" their loyalty. My animal-magnetism speaks for me, and if they are too bigoted or ignorant to listen, then let them join Barth and his cronies in their jealous determination to suppress my discovery. Of course, I can understand Barth's terror of the truth being made public. That highly-respected old fraud wasn't able to make the girl see. And I did. (*He pauses*) I'm a little disappointed in you, though, Anna. Your lack of loyalty——

Frau Mesmer I support you in public.

Mesmer And you think that sufficient?

Pause

Frau Mesmer It has to be. I can't live the sort of life you now demand.

Mesmer But you, at least, have proof of my ability. Your son is married to

one of my most celebrated successes. Franzl Oesterlin was in a——
Frau Mesmer I haven't your dedication, Anton. And it's a bit late for me to change. My life has always consisted of those frivolous activities you now so heartily deplore. While we were able to move in parallel lines, enjoying our own pursuits, all was well, but now the lines have become tangled, and I find myself the target for ostracism and ridicule.
Mesmer It's me they ridicule, not you.
Frau Mesmer (*shaking her head*) I'm the ageing, frigid wife, who drove you into the arms of a girl young enough to be your daughter. Oh, some of them pity me, but they all think it my own fault for having married a younger man.
Mesmer At our age, what's ten years?
Frau Mesmer Some think twenty. Some think me as old as the pyramids.
Mesmer (*smiling*) Poor Anna. You should have more sense than to listen to their vicious tongues.
Frau Mesmer And you should have had more sense than to have given them cause.
Mesmer I can't stop my work just to accommodate——
Frau Mesmer Can't you see the next step? You'll succeed in getting yourself expelled from the faculty—that very body you've been trying to impress over all these years.
Mesmer They wouldn't dare!
Frau Mesmer Who'd want to be treated by you then? What would you do?

Pause

Mesmer There are other cities . . . where people are less prejudiced.
Frau Mesmer You'd move away?
Mesmer I've been thinking of Paris for some time now.

Pause

Frau Mesmer I don't think I want to leave Vienna.
Mesmer What is there left here?
Frau Mesmer Friends, such as I still have. Maybe I am as old as the pyramids. I don't feel capable of starting a completely new life. Or would it be a new life? Maybe a continuation of this, in a different setting. What if Paris rejected you? What then? London? Rome? Travelling the world, like gypsies?
Mesmer (*cuttingly*) I agree, it would interfere with your soirées, somewhat.
Frau Mesmer (*lightly*) Oh, I believe even the Parisians occasionally make merry. But would I?

Pause

Mesmer You must make your own decisions, Anna. I shall certainly make mine when the time comes.

The Lights dim and come up on the coffee house, where Frau Schwartz and Frau Paradies are chatting

Frau Schwartz And they talk about daughters being a comfort! Mine's anything but a comfort. An embarrassment. I mean, one can forgive her the size and spots, but not her tendency to flirt with anything in trousers. Any other husband would thrash her to within an inch of her life. But, of course, he'd need to stay sober enough to remain on his feet for that, wouldn't he? How's *your* daughter?

Frau Paradies Flourishing! Very happy, and pleased to be back home. We're already arranging a concert tour, starting in Prague.

Frau Schwartz Sounds wonderful. Do excuse me for a moment. I must see what that fat idler's doing in the kitchen.

She rushes off

Frau Paradies remains, sipping her coffee

The Lights come up on the Paradies house. Herr Paradies sits deep in thought

Maria enters and feels her way to the piano. She is blind. She begins to play

Herr Paradies You know I'd send you back to him today ... were it not that your mother becomes ill and screams at the very suggestion. (*He pauses*) She gets upset so easily. We both do, I suppose. It's the influence he had over you. Made you almost hate us. (*He pauses*) I'm sorry, Maria.
Maria I don't mind, Papa. Really I don't.

Pause

Herr Paradies Before ... you didn't know what you were missing.

Pause

Maria Sight seemed ... almost abnormal. Uncomfortable. (*She pauses*) I remember the stars. But little else. (*She pauses*) I've never needed to see.
Herr Paradies You don't want to go back to him?
Maria No. (*She pauses*) I'm not saying that to put you at ease. My sight was only part of what he gave me. The minor part. I no longer have fits, do I? I'm not even afraid of you and Mama killing each other any more. Oh, when I first came back I was agitated, and felt like running away ... (*she pauses*) ... then, when my sight began to go again, that was when I became calm. That was when I really came home. Home to the comfortable darkness I'd always known.

The Lights dim on Maria and her father

Frau Schwartz returns from the kitchen, and sweeps across to Frau Paradies

Frau Schwartz Sitting there picking her spots, and dreaming of men, as usual. Revolting creature. So your daughter's ready for concerts again, is she?
Frau Paradies And very excited about it, too.
Frau Schwartz I can imagine she is. But I thought she'd lost her ability to play?
Frau Paradies Another of Mesmer's lies. An excuse to keep her there.
Frau Schwartz Did you hear that he's leaving Vienna?

Frau Paradies Once people discover their tricks, they have to move on, don't they? I'm surprised he managed to deceive everyone for as long as he did.
Frau Schwartz How's her sight?
Frau Paradies Sight?
Frau Schwartz Your daughter.
Frau Paradies Blind as ever, poor girl.
Frau Schwartz But you told me she could see!
Frau Paradies That's what we thought at the time. Oh, he was able to convince even her own parents—the charlatan! But it was all a cruel trick. An illusion. She's never been able to see at all. (*She pauses*) But she's home now, thank God, with those who really care for her.

The Lights dim

EPILOGUE

Paris 1784. A continuation of the Prologue

Maria I knew you were here in Paris. You came here that same year. I didn't think you'd want to see me again, though.
Mesmer Why should you think that?
Maria One of your failures... partly the reason for your leaving Vienna...
Mesmer Had you come back to me you wouldn't have been a "failure" as you put it.
Maria I didn't want to.
Mesmer It was your father who——
Maria Not his fault. I think I could have persuaded him.
Frau Paradies (*off*) Maria-Theresa!
Maria Even Mama. But I didn't want to. I must go to her. Don't worry about me. I can still hear music. And applause. (*She begins to move away*) How is dear Frau Mesmer?
Mesmer Well, so I'm told. (*After a pause*) I've not seen her since leaving Vienna.
Maria I'm sorry.
Mesmer Why? She couldn't see beyond her next "soirée".
Maria As you can't see beyond your next "miracle cure" and I can't "see" beyond my next concert.
Frau Paradies (*off; more distant*) Maria-Theresa!
Maria Good-night, Herr Doctor.
Mesmer Good-night, Fräulein.

Maria goes

The Lights dim

CURTAIN

FURNITURE AND PROPERTY LIST

PROLOGUE

On stage: Nil

Personal: **Maria**: cane

ACT I

On stage: Frau Schwartz's coffee house:
Tables. *On one:* playing cards, paper, pencil
Chairs
Counter. *On it:* various bottles including brandy, glasses

Paradies house:
Sofa. *On it:* cushions
Chairs. *On them:* cushions
Piano
Piano stool
Table. *On it:* bowl of flowers, dish of sweets

Mesmer house:
Desk
Chairs
Table. *On it:* small bell
Piano. *On top:* sheet music
Piano stool
Books

Props required: Coffee house:
Cup of coffee (**Frau Paradies**) } page 19
Duster (**Frau Schwartz**)

Paradies house:
Book (**Herr Paradies**, page 7)
Letter (**Herr Paradies**, page 16)
Cup of coffee (**Herr Paradies**) } page 22
Various hats (**Frau Paradies**)

Mesmer house:
Black wooden wand (**Mesmer**, page 17)
Bandages over eyes (**Maria**, page 17)
Notes (**Mesmer**, page 21)
Handkerchief, book, wine-glass, vase (**Mesmer**, page 23)

ACT II

Set: Cups of coffee on table in coffee house
Different coloured objects in Mesmer house

The Charlatan

Props required: Coffee house:
Cup of coffee (**Frau Schwartz**, page 27)
Cup of coffee (**Frau Schwartz**, page 34)
Cup of coffee (**Frau Paradies**, page 53)

Paradies house:
Blanket (**Frau Paradies**)
Writing paper, pen (**Herr Paradies**) } page 48

Mesmer house:
Letters (**Frau Mesmer**, page 45)

Personal: **Barth**: money in pocket

EPILOGUE

On stage: Nil

Personal: **Maria**: cane

LIGHTING PLOT

Property fittings required: nil

1 exterior, 3 interiors—a coffee house, the Paradies house, the Mesmer house (composite setting)

PROLOGUE. Evening

To open: Dim, shadowy lighting

Cue 1	**Maria**: "... offer me in return?" *Fade lights*	(Page 2)

ACT I

To open: Lighting on coffee house

Cue 2	**Barth**: "We think not." *Cross-fade to Paradies house*	(Page 7)
Cue 3	**Frau Paradies**: "... alone for a minute." *Cross-fade to coffee house*	(Page 10)
Cue 4	**Stoerck**: "And with 'unorthodox' methods, too." He smiles *Cross-fade to Mesmer house*	(Page 11)
Cue 5	**Maria**: "... one's whole existence ..." *Cross-fade to Paradies house*	(Page 16)
Cue 6	**Frau Paradies** sweeps out *Cross-fade to Mesmer house—dim lighting*	(Page 17)
Cue 7	**Maria** slowly reaches out to touch book *Cross-fade to coffee house*	(Page 19)
Cue 8	**Frau Paradies**: "... in all probability." *Cross-fade to Mesmer house*	(Page 21)
Cue 9	**Mesmer** watches his wife exit, then returns to his notes *Cross-fade to Paradies house*	(Page 22)
Cue 10	**Herr Paradies**: "I hate cold coffee." *Cross-fade to Mesmer house—dim lighting*	(Page 22)
Cue 11	**Maria** goes to piano and begins playing *Bring up lighting on Paradies house*	(Page 24)
Cue 12	**Frau Paradies** pops a sweet in her mouth and picks up hats *Fade lights on Paradies house*	(Page 26)
Cue 13	**Maria**: "... happier ... as I was." *Fade lights*	(Page 26)

The Charlatan

ACT II

To open:	Lighting on coffee house	
Cue 14	**Stoerck**: "... my hours in exile ..." They laugh *Cross-fade to Mesmer house*	(Page 28)
Cue 15	**Mesmer**: "... to see you out." *Cross-fade to coffee house*	(Page 34)
Cue 16	**Barth** (*raising his eyebrows*): "Do we?" *Cross-fade to Paradies house*	(Page 35)
Cue 17	**Frau Paradies**: "... how a mother feels." She storms out *Cross-fade to coffee house*	(Page 37)
Cue 18	**Frau Paradies** goes, **Frau Schwartz** smiles blissfully *Cross-fade to Mesmer house*	(Page 40)
Cue 19	**Frau Paradies** covers her face and cries *Cross-fade to Paradies house*	(Page 43)
Cue 20	**Barth**: "... you or your wife." *Bring up light on Mesmer*	(Page 43)
Cue 21	**Mesmer** goes *Fade light on his area*	(Page 45)
Cue 22	**Barth**: "We'll see." *Cross-fade to Mesmer house*	(Page 45)
Cue 23	**Mesmer** goes quickly; his wife stares at the letters *Cross-fade to Paradies house*	(Page 48)
Cue 24	**Herr Paradies**: "... we'll see what happens." *Cross-fade to coffee house*	(Page 49)
Cue 25	**Stoerck**: "... that would involve." *Cross-fade to Mesmer house*	(Page 50)
Cue 26	**Mesmer**: "... when the time comes." *Cross-fade to coffee house*	(Page 52)
Cue 27	**Frau Schwartz** rushes off; **Frau Paradies** remains, sipping her coffee *Bring up lights on Paradies house*	(Page 53)
Cue 28	**Maria**: "... darkness I'd always known." *Fade lights on Paradies house*	(Page 53)
Cue 29	**Frau Paradies**: "... who really care for her." *Fade lights*	(Page 54)

EPILOGUE

To open:	Dim, shadowy lighting	
Cue 30	**Maria** goes *Fade lights*	(Page 55)

EFFECTS PLOT

PROLOGUE

Cue 1   Before CURTAIN rises   (Page 1)
Final bars of Mozart's Piano Concerto in B flat, K456, followed by applause

ACT I

Cue 2   Lights cross-fade to Mesmer house   (Page 21)
Music—string quartet in background

ACT II

Cue 3   **Frau Schwartz**: "... a rather unusual colour ..."   (Page 28)
Crash of china, off

EPILOGUE

No cues

MADE AND PRINTED IN GREAT BRITAIN BY
LATIMER TREND & COMPANY LTD PLYMOUTH